CW01647442

Preachers' Gath

Preaching Spiritual Warfare

Derek Newton

November 2023

Preaching Spiritual Warfare

Derek Newton

Published by Nigel Barge
Strathlachlan, Cairndow, Scotland PA27 8BU

ISBN 978-1-912209-87-3

Website:
https://hearingtheword.org.uk

Copyright © Derek Newton 2023

Derek Newton has asserted his economic and moral rights under the Copyright, Designs and Patents Act 1988, to be identified as the author of this work, and compiler of the quotations cited. All rights reserved.

However,...
This work is made available under the
Creative Commons Licence 4.0 International, version 6,
i.e.: Attribution-NonCommercial-NoDerivatives CC BY-NC-ND.

This licence allows readers to download text by Derek Newton and share it with others, as long as they credit the author, but they cannot change it in any way or use it commercially.

To view the terms of the Licence in simplified form, follow this link:
http://creativecommons.org/licenses/by-nc-nd/6.0/?ref=chooser-v1
It provides a further link to the actual licence in legal terms.

Scripture Quotations taken from
THE HOLY BIBLE, NEW INTERNATIONAL VERSION
Copyright © 1973, 1978, 1984, 2011 by Biblica, Inc® The International Bible Society. Used by permission of Hodder and Stoughton Ltd.
A member of the Hodder Headline Plc Group. All rights reserved

"NIV" is a registered trademark of International Bible Society.
UK trademark no. 1448790

Contents

Preachers' Gatherings

Between 2016 and 2023, preachers and their spouses were invited to a good hotel in Aviemore or Polmont, Scotland, twice a year. The Gatherings, which ran from Monday morning to after lunch on Tuesday, provided good food, brilliant Bible teaching, prayer for each other, wonderful fellowship and relaxation, all as a free gift by a Trust fund. This material was delivered at Gatherings in November 2023.

Foreword to the Series

Many of us believe that *'All scripture is God-breathed and is useful for teaching, rebuking, correcting and training in righteousness…'* (2 Timothy 3:16)

Such are the extreme demands and time pressure on church leaders, however, many of us avoid preaching from some of its more difficult parts.

During the Preachers' Gatherings, Derek Newton and Peter White gave teaching on Books of the Bible that are often neglected in our churches. Their remit was to equip preachers, over 4 hours, to deliver a series of sermons on the book in question, to start in 2 weeks' time. A tall order!

This task took them months of time in preparation. They read widely and produced booklets reflecting that. In these, they dealt with the exegesis of the text, incorporated the views of others and gave their own perspective of its meaning. On top of all of that, they gave suggestions on how it might be broken down and preached.

My testimony is, that over 30 years of ministry, I never found any teaching or resource like theirs. They enabled and gave courage to a journeyman preacher to attempt to teach his folk parts of the Bible that he had never had the nerve or the time to address.

For that, I am very grateful to Derek and Peter and commend their teaching to any who understand the imperative of opening up the whole Bible in their ministry, but are daunted by the prospect.

Nigel Barge
February 2024

INTRODUCTION: Are Witchcraft and Warfare Real?

See **Jonathan Burnside**, *Covert power: unmasking the world of witchcraft.* Cambridge Papers, Dec 2010.

John Wesley in 1768 wrote, "It is true…that the English in general, and indeed most of the men of learning in Europe, have given up all accounts of witches and apparitions as mere old wives' fables…. I willingly take this opportunity of entering my solemn protest against this violent compliment which so many that believe the Bible pay to those who do not believe it… The giving up of witchcraft is in effect giving up the Bible".

Burnside says, "Witchcraft is often present in society because it expresses something deep-seated in our broken humanity, namely, our desire to carve out a space where we can make things happen apart from God. The seriousness of witchcraft tends to be overlooked both in materialist societies, such as the UK, that pretend spiritual activity doesn't exist, and in societies that actively collude with supernatural powers, such as South Africa. The Bible presents a challenge to both sorts of worldview because it recongnises there is a spiritual world – but one which is subject to Jesus Christ's authority".

Burnside uses the term 'witchcraft' loosely in his paper to refer to engagement with the spirit world in ways that, in practice, ignore God's reality. He writes "The subject is important because the unseen spiritual realm is more powerful than we can imagine, or deal with…rebellious spiritual powers are dangerous". Witchcraft is found across the globe but is most easily seen in Africa, Asia and the Caribbean/Latin America. The unknown 'spiritual world' makes people feel insecure, obsessed and fearful! The reality however is that occult practices are widespread in the West, especially in Celtic, Scandinavian and Western Europe, and indeed in Britain, seen in the many shops re tarot, crystal and palmistry. Burnside says "Overt witchcraft is practised in modern Britain…. Every Anglican diocese has a dedicated exorcist…. Witchcraft is real – and the UK is only a whisker away from a neopagan resurgence".

There is a basic difference of worldview here. Thus, South African witch-doctors believe that the spirit world exists; on the other side, the materialist worldview claims the spirit world does not exist. Those who engage in the spirit world do so in order to seek knowledge of people and circumstances to help or harm them, to gain control and manipulation over people and to deal with their fears over death. Materialists would simply not understand this.

Herein lie weaknesses in both directions of thought. The spiritists believe that humans can access the spirit world by various means and control people and events in the material world. They deny the reality of God. Mediums can access the spiritual world but spiritists simply ignore that Jesus exercises authority over this spiritual world. The opposite error is that the materialist worldview does not accept the existence of a spirit world. Sometimes, materialists reject all claims to spiritual reality. The Bible challenges *both worldviews*!

How? Burnside writes "Unlike the materialists, it affirms there is a spiritual dimension. But that does not mean we are being irrational and should prostrate ourselves to spirits. For unlike practitioners of witchcraft, the Bible holds out a Christ-centred vision of reality: one in which Jesus is in charge of the spirit (and the material) world. Both materialists and spiritists need to find the basis of reality in Christ".

Burnside then continues his argument as follows – "Nevertheless, although the spiritist and materialist worldviews are rejected by Scripture as mistaken, there are also Christian versions of these mistakes".

a) Christian versions of the *spiritist* worldview – Some elements of the church accept the reality of the spiritual world but connect with it in unbiblical ways eg some label certain people as 'witches' but then offer 'deliverance' – for a charge! Also witchcraft involvement is common among many Christians in Africa, described by Joseph K'Amolo as "holding the Bible by day, seeking oracles by night". When the church adopts a spiritist orientation worldview, it does not address witchcraft, because it doesn't witness to Christ's authority effectively.

b) Christian versions of the *materialist* worldview – When the church takes up a materialist worldview, it 'despiritualises the Christian life, ie Satan drops out, angels vanish, and God's active involvement in human issues gets downplayed. When this happens, the church fails to offer redemption via appropriate healing, prayer or exorcisms, if appropriate, and it fails to equip people with spiritual weaponry. The fastest-growing churches in much of the global South are those that deal with human fears and equip their people to deal with spiritual forces. In contrast to this trend, mainline Anglican and Baptist churches sometimes ignore the reality of spiritual warfare, but suffer from slower growth.

What is a biblical perspective on witches and warfare?

The biblical view is unique and exclusive, because it places all spiritual authority in Yahweh, Israel's God. This forbids the gaining of any supernatural power and knowledge from any other source whatsoever. See God's creation of spiritual beings through Christ and for Him in Colossians 1:16; Ezek 1:5-14; Rev 4:6-8. Christ is sovereign over evil angels ('demons') who are rebelling against God and imposing their evil influences in the world, under Satan's leading. *Jesus fully recognised the reality of these evil forces.* (Lk 8:2) Christians are fighting such powers (Eph 6:12). Yet the amazing truth is that these powers, powerful, created beings, are all under Christ's authority – see Jesus' ministry in dealing with them (Mk 5:1-20) and Jesus' ongoing work by His Spirit through the Church (Acts 16:16-18; Phil 2:9-11). Satan absolutely *must* bow down to this Christ!! Believers must relate to unseen or seen powers only out of a secure relationship, from which we know, trust and love this God in Christ.

This is why witchcraft is out of the question for Christians, because it tries to connect with the spiritual world apart from God. Witchcraft is the absolute opposite to spiritual intimacy, which is why manipulation and control kills all relationships. It isolates and dehumanises, doing great damage. It destroys human character and treads on the value of other people. Read of God's protective power in Psalm 91, based on His faithfulness and our intimacy with Him. Burnside writes, "We do not need to know the future, or control events, or fear death, because we have intimacy with God, who is the end of all things". Deut 18:9-19 stresses the vast difference between witchcraft (manipulation) and prophecy (intimacy), rooted in Israel's deliverance from Egypt. *See* Ex 19:6; Amos 3:2; Mt 22:32

'Creative spirituality' = truth, intimacy, life, adventure.
'Destructive spirituality' = deception, control, death, fear.

For example, Saul sought out the witch of Endor to connect with the spirit of Samuel. Saul lacked intimacy with God and thus turned to necromancy in an experience of destructive spirituality – see 1 Sam 28:8ff and 1 Chron 10:13-14. Saul is spiritually dead, so that only the dead can speak to him, but Saul is actually unable to manipulate Samuel to achieve his own purposes. Even here, God is in control. Samuel condemns the ritual (vv 15-16). Samuel uses God's name seven times in his message and focuses on Saul's loss of divine help! It is very dangerous to try to speak to the spirit world outside of God's authority. Saul fears death, but his use of witchcraft gives no help!

We and indeed our wider society need to keep the protective covering of Christianity. To lose this will guarantee utter disaster!

Amidst the technological Western world, there are those materialists who do have an interest in connecting with the supernatural. In these different worldviews, there is a still deeper level of application. Burnside starts his argument as follows:

In Matthew's Sermon on the Mount, Jesus deals with elements of biblical law that readers and hearers feel they have upheld, eg 'Do not murder'! This is then related to heart attitudes, namely 'do not cherish anger against another person'. (Matt 5:22) Those who felt themselves innocent of murder could in fact exhibit or possess the underlying thoughts of a murderer!

Similarly, we might feel we have avoided the practice of witchcraft, but may nevertheless have owned the attitudes of witchcraft. How? Because witchcraft starts with our wish to carve out an area or space in which we might try to make things happen without God. The manipulation of spiritual powers for our own purposes is surely a kind of human pride that tries to place ourselves in the place of God. In various ways, we try to manipulate events and people to meet our own ends and desires, without complete trust in the Lord God. We enjoy a life that consists of power and control, at the same time as denying God's control and power over the tiny details of daily life. We may not be sorcerers or wizards, but are we using subliminal advertising or clever spin-doctoring! Hidden persuasion is widespread and we absorb messages and values from soap stories. Often we are unaware. We can use 'people management skills' and manipulate people as we discover which buttons to press so as to influence them! We can unwittingly be influenced by secular values to subtly seek power and control, without realizing what we are actually doing! This is a form of witchcraft actually. We are in danger of being powerfully controlled and seeking to powerfully control others.

Just how do we actually function, perhaps unconsciously, as church members, deacons, elders and yes...ministers and leaders, even in the midst of what we might feel is simply and solely normal, everyday living?! This can happen in a kind of 'covert witchcraft', in which we may fail to respect other people or treat them in an honest, transparent way. Knowledge and control can become substitutes for true intimacy. This can involve getting information about a person in order to exploit, damage or manipulate that person for our own ends. We do this without full trust in God or genuine respect for those other people! They parallel witchcraft by sharing the same attitudes of witchcraft. This is covert power – amidst the ordinary things of life (2 Cor 4:2). We must live and steer wisely in the biblical middle between spiritism and materialism, finding intimacy, light and life.

SPIRITUAL WARFARE and…

1 …its Origin and Relation to Evil, Satan and Sin

With great honesty, the Rev John Piper has tackled this knotty subject area of *How did the first sin of Satan come about?* In an interview, and answer to a church-member's enquiry, Piper has admitted that he has not yet reached a satisfactory answer to this question! (John Piper, *The Origin of Satan and* Sin.) He does affirm that "The Bible opens not with the beginning of evil, but with the presence of unexplained evil. Man is created innocent, and the serpent is already there. The serpent is deceitful and manifestly opposed to the God of creation. That is where the Bible begins". The Bible does not seem to explain just how Satan became evil. Piper is aware of 'hints' that Satan was a perfect angel created by God – see Jude 6 on angels who strayed from their proper place. Piper says he can accept that Satan was created good but fell from his appropriate place. He does not think that 'evil' and 'God' are *both* eternal and ultimate realities. Rather, he believes that God and His absolute goodness, wisdom and power are the only ultimate, eternal realities. Piper does not know just how Satan became evil and does not believe that Satan's free will explains why he committed his first sin. We simply do not know the answer to this great mystery, admits John Piper. Why on earth would Satan decide to become a rebel against God? Piper has no answer to this.

What Piper *does affirm* is the absolute sovereignty of God. His plan includes things He "more or less causes directly – things He more or less permits indirectly". God is able to allow to happen some things that He actually hates! Eg. He planned the crucifixion of Jesus (Acts 4:27-28). That murder was massively sinful, yet God planned it at every stage! This is indeed a mystery but the Bible seems to allow that God is sovereign over all sin, and yet God never sins! Piper accepts one clue/indicator/ pointer – the prophet Isaiah in 63:17 cries to the people "O Lord, why do you make us wander from your ways and harden our hearts, so that we fear you not? Return for the sake of your servants, the tribes of your heritage." This is indeed staggering. Isaiah sees God as the ultimate cause of our wandering into sin. How is that possible? That verse seems to say that God's *absence* caused us to sin. A few verses later, in Isaiah 64:7, Isaiah then says " There is no one who calls upon your name, who rouses himself to take hold of you; for you have hidden your face from us, and have made us melt in the hands of our iniquities." So again, it is the hiding of his face which explains the sin! Piper admits that this is not a guaranteed explanation of sin, but in some way,

God hid and covered His glory from Satan and that somehow, in this concealing of God's glory, Satan begins in his heart, to prefer himself rather than the God who has hidden his glory.

The Bible teaches the sovereignty of God over all things, including sin, and God Himself is *never* a sinner. Thus, thinks Piper, "God may be able to govern the presence and absence of sin not by direct, active agency, but by concealing Himself". Piper offers an illustration of this – he recalls probably Jonathan Edwards who noted a difference between the way light is caused at 3 o'clock in the afternoon by the shining of the sun and the way the shadows are caused by the blocking of that sun by the tree – though it is the light of the *sun* that causes both the brightness of the day and the shadows under the tree! Even so, Piper admits to his own ignorance of how the very first sin in this universe actually happened!

This mysterious question has been explored in considerable detail by Michael Green in his book *I Believe in Satan's Downfall* Eerdmans. He concedes that we have enough knowledge in Scripture to be able to love and serve God, but also to fight against our chief Enemy, Satan, who Green describes as being "expert at covering his traces". Indeed! Green concludes that Piper's question on the mystery of Satan's origin and influence in the midst of God's perfect world, has only three possible answers –

a) Some take the view that the term 'Satan' is drawn from poem, story or myth to explain the bewildering issue of the existence of evil, disease and death in a world that was intended by God to be perfect! However, Satan and demons are actually hostile powers operating in a world that is threatened by them. These beings appear frequently in the biblical material, though we still do not get an actual explanation of the origin of evil itself.

b) Similar to the idea of a Government and Opposition, many hold the position that this twofold political division explains the opposition that seems to exist in the world between good and evil. Biblical truth however does not offer dualism or the idea of the existence of equal or opposite powers led by God and Satan. This 'political' perspective also fails to explain the actual origin of evil itself.

c) The more traditional view of the devil is that he was actually a creature made by God, but which became obsessed with pride and rebelled against God and as a result lost his place in the universe and became the arch Enemy of the Godhead. So this Biblical position views Satan as a divine, but now fallen, creature (Isaiah 45:6f; Amos 3:6). This strange pattern is perhaps most vividly seen in the Book of Job in which Satan is seen as a 'son of God' who has to appear periodically before the Lord God, to get instructions from Him. Satan has the freedom to insult and accuse Job in the presence of God (Job 1:9). Satan is even allowed to attack and damage Job in the matter of his possessions and then in devastating Job in his own person (Job 1:12; 2:5-6). Yet even in the extremities of Job's pain and anguish, God sets limits on the freedom of Satan to hurt Job. The actual life of Job is not within Satan's freedom to take. Satan is reminded by this that actually he is a creature and is finally and ultimately subject to God's overruling and overriding power. God alone has the overarching knowledge, power and control that make Him Lord of the Universe.

So then, amidst the uncertainty about the origin of evil and the reason(s) for Satan's first sin, what can we say with certainty? In this universe, there are two kingdoms at war with each other – the angelic Kingdom of God and the demonic kingdom of darkness. This Spiritual Warfare is being engaged on two levels – the supernatural or spiritual, and the natural or material level. In the western rationalistic world, we tend to dismiss the supernatural or spirit level of warfare, yet both are real. Satan gained dominion over the earth through the fall of humanity. Satan assaults Jesus in the wilderness and claims that the kingdoms of the world belong to Satan. Jesus begins to make war on Satan on every level, through His miracles over demons, death, disease and nature and through the preaching of the gospel (Luke 4:18-19). Both kingdoms are in conflict over the souls of humanity. Satan's drive and goal is to pull humanity into eternal damnation. His work began in the heavenly realm, extended to earth and humanity in Eden and using the fall of humanity, continues across the globe, until Christ returns to consummate and complete His Kingdom. Satan employs and infiltrates economic, political and religious systems to entrap people. Jesus destroys Satan's work by his death and rising, and by the preaching of this!

Spiritual Warfare and ...
2 ...the Names & Natures of Satan – a Biblical exploration

NAMES OF SATAN

Scripture uses a wide range of names for 'Satan' and demonic forces. A name in Scripture is not a mere label, but is an indicator of character.

1. **SATAN** – The Greek *Satanas* means 'adversary' or 'slanderer' ie one who tries to trigger rebellion against God. Satan is the one who seeks for opportunities to express his hatred of God and Christ (Mt 4:10; Mk 1:13), of God's people (Lk 22:31, Acts 5:3) and of humankind (Mt 16:23, Lk 13:16, Acts 26:18). Satan accuses us before God and seeks to claim that we can never be acceptable to God! In the OT, we find three key references to 'Satan' –

a) in Job 1:6 'the satan' occurs as the accuser/tormenter of suffering Job .

b) in Zech 3:1ff 'the satan' mocks the devastation of Jerusalem and aims false charges/lies against Joshua, who was high priest at the time of the restoration after the Babylonian exile. The Lord God cleanses Joshua with the promise of rule in God's household, as long as Joshua keeps the divine commands. This also looks forward to another 'Joshua' who is accused, in the form of Christian believers, day and night before God in Rev 12:10. This accusing role of satan also fails miserably in Revelation;

c) in 1 Chron 21:1, Satan – included as a proper name - tempts David to number the people and boast of his military strength. By this time of the Chronicles, following the exile experience, Satan's evil character was coming more to the fore and more readily recognised.

2. **SON OF GOD** – This very unexpected title for Satan occasionally appears in Scripture and shows the link with Satan's origin. Thus, in Job 1:6 we read "Now there was a day when...the sons of God came to present themselves before the Lord, and Satan came also with them." This term "Sons of God" usually refers to angels in the OT and we are told here that when the sons of God came to the heavenly court, Satan was one of them. This points to Satan's origin ie. originally he was God's creation and he remains God's devil, but subject to God's ultimate control.

   This title links Satan to his origin but also in a sense to his function as **'TEMPTER',** in which he seeks to push people into the same sort of estrangement from God that he himself chose when he fell away from his creator, God. (Lk 4; Matt 4:3; 1 Thess 3:5)

3. **DEVIL** – The Greek *diabolos* means 'Accuser' and 'Slanderer', with the aim of destroying people before God and one another. We read of him as accuser in Job 1-2, liar in John 8:44 and murderer in 1 John 3:12. There is indeed one 'devil', but many demons (Greek *daimonia*).

4. **BEELZEBUB** and **BELIAR** – 'Beliar' is another name that is once attached to the 'devil' by Paul in 2 Cor 6:15. This name may be just the same as 'Belial' which was commonly used in the intertestamental era for 'Satan' and meaning 'the Worthless One'. 'Baalzebub' appears as god of Ekron, consulted by Ahaziah, king of Israel, during his last illness (2 Kings 1:1-6,16). To the Jews, 'Baalzebub' was the Lord of the whole realm of the occult, rooted in the Greek *belos* meaning flying thing or missile. This term also appears as 'Beelzebul' (Mt 10:25, 12:26, Lk 11:15) or 'Beelzebub', meaning 'Lord of the Flies' or 'Lord of filth' but most likely meaning 'Lord of the dwelling'. The NT links Beelzebub with Satan as 'prince of the demons' (Mt 12:24,27) and as 'master of the house' (Mt 10:25). It clearly is a reference to the devil. The focus is on the strength of Satan once he gets hold of a person's life! He indeed becomes 'Lord'.

5. **DRAGON** and **SERPENT** – Satan is a highly skilled and powerful tempter, thus earning him the title 'that old serpent' (Rev 12:9 linked with Genesis 3). The 'serpent' is connected with, and indeed identified as, Satan in various contexts – skulking (Job 26:13); poisonous (Ps 58:4, 1 Cor 10:9, Rev 9:19); treacherous (Gen 49:17, 2 Cor 11:3); subtlety and cause of chaos (Gen 3). Other appearances in Rev 12:9,14,15; 20:2; 1 Tim 2:13ff; Rom 16:20, Rev 12:9, 20:2. Many ancient religions view the dragon as the arch Enemy of all that is good, the ultimate in evil across the Ancient Near East. John in his Revelation relates the 'great red dragon' in Rev 12:3 and has picked this up from the beast of Daniel's prophecy in Daniel 7:7ff. The numbers seven and ten signify perfection and completion in perpetrating widespread, though ultimately limited, evil! Dragon also means and describes the devil in Rev 12:3,4,7,9,13,16,17; 13:2,4,11; 16:13; 20:2.

6. **LUCIFER** – This term means 'shining one' and 'light-bearer' and makes a number of appearances – *Isa 14:12,* identified with the king of Babylon, who had set himself among the gods; *Luke 10:18* and *Rev 9:1* the name 'Lucifer' is applied here to Satan; *2 Cor 11:14,* Satan shows himself as an 'angel of light'!; *Rev 22:16*, Christ Himself is the true holder of this title in his glory.

7. **THE EVIL ONE** – Satan is called the Antichrist and as such embodies opposition to the Christian Godhead – see 1 John 4:1ff.

Satan is the ultimate Enemy of humankind (Lk 10:19). Satan is the one who accuses all who turn to Christ and away from darkness (1 Peter 5:8; Acts 26:18). Satan seeks our downfall, either as a 'roaring lion' to devour us (1 Peter 5:8) or as an attractive 'angel of light' to deceive us. (2 Cor 10:14) In short, he is the 'evil one' (Mt 19:38, 13:19,38; 2 Thess 3:3). The Matthew reference in the Lord's Prayer is most probably to be translated as, 'Deliver us from *the Evil One'*. He desires the worst possible outcome for all human lives and eternities!

8. **DESTROYER** – Satan's character is also highly destructive – see the Apollyon, meaning 'The Destroyer', in Rev 9:11. This takes us back to Gen 3 where sin and death both enter this world through the Fall that had been engineered by our Enemy, Satan. John 8:44 does not mean that Satan randomly kills people, for his power is definitely limited by God (Job 2:6), but it does indicate the fear of death that Satan loves to inject into humanity. Physical death *is* an element of God's curse on sin, but it is true that Satan has already rendered humanity as captured slaves who are all spiritually 'dead through trespasses and sins' (Eph 2:1ff). That's why physical death is the 'last enemy', but the latter, plus all the other works of Satan, will finally be destroyed by Christ (1 John 3:8). The sting of death will finally be removed. (1 Cor 15:54f)

9. **PRINCE OF THE POWER OF THE AIR** – Ephesians 2:2. Ancient peoples viewed the abyss as the final destination of Satan and his angels (Lk 8:31; Rev 20:2) but they saw the air as the area of Satanic activity, between earth and heaven. Eph. 6:12 confirms this view of Satan as head of the world rulers of this present darkness, spiritual host of wickedness in the heavenly places. Satan is very powerful and does have an empire + servants (Rev 12:4,9) + world rulers + control over the power of darkness + spiritual chains with which to enslave people.

10. **RULER OF THIS WORLD** – This title for Satan appears three times in John's Gospel (12:31, 14:30, 16:11). Also referred to in Eph 6:12. He is also called 'the god of this world' (2 Cor 4:4) and in 1 John 5:19 it is recorded that 'the whole world lies in the arms of/in the wicked one'. In the temptations of Jesus, it seems that somehow Satan is claiming a special relationship with/to this world. Some scholars wonder whether Satan had been given some sort of special responsibility or authority over this world before he fell and rebelled against the Godhead. This is mere speculation but it is worth reflecting on the cry in Revelation 12:12 following Satan's fall from heaven – "Rejoice then, O Heaven, and you that dwell therein! But woe to you, O earth and sea, for the devil has come down to you in great wrath, because he knows his time is short".

Spiritual Warfare and…

3 …its Roots in Scripture: the Chief Features of Satan's Natures

Prof TF Torrance made the following comment in *Apocalypse Today,* p.95: "It is precisely because the Devil and all his minions have been so utterly defeated that the earth is thrown into such turmoil and trouble. That decisive defeat becomes apparent as all the powers of spiritual evil, dislodged by the Cross, fall upon the earth and gather, by subtle deception, the prides and passions and lust of men, and direct them against the Kingdom of God as it is being enacted in history".

Let's start with the crucial, critical, but controversial and strangely neglected account of Satan's fundamental strategy as revealed in Genesis Chapter 3. There are vital lessons to be learned here. This Garden of Eden was a gift from God for humanity – a place of peace and purity that came to a disastrous and tragic end! Temptation came to Eve in an unexpected way and it came from Satan in disguise as a plausible serpent. Satan does have a clear plan to trigger disobedience against God, and thereby to gain control over men and women! This would guarantee the breaking of their relationship with God, in the way that Satan's own relationship with God had been smashed by self-desire and pride. Satan thus sets out to work against the God-created elements of humanity's key parts.

Satan works on human, physical appetites that are fundamentally good in themselves but are prone to be damaged by Enemy attack, namely human desire for sleep, sex, strength, drink and food. The results can be gluttony, alcoholism, laziness, violence, power, greed, materialism and immorality. Yet, much of humanity scoffs at the real dangers inherent in the massive warnings of basic Genesis 3 truth! At the same time as his physical focus for temptation, Satan pinpoints the human mind of Eve, as he aims to raise doubt and confusion in her thinking. The Serpent encourages her to doubt the goodness of God – "Did God really say, 'You must not eat from any tree in the garden?'" Clearly this question does not represent what God actually said. This inaccurate version is not only false, but implies that God is a mean person who tries to limit permissible human pleasures. At the same time, the Serpent is causing the woman to doubt the truth of God's Word. This leads people to wonder whether God's Word is actually valid and relevant today and whether this Word is still to be considered as our faithful guide in all matters of faith and practice today. At the same time, the Serpent is undermining in the woman's mind the holiness of God with his suggestion, "You will not die", as if God actually lacks moral standards and will turn a blind eye to our acts of disobedience. This brings God down to little more than a human level of behavior and opens the door for humanity to ignore human conscience and divine Word, without any negative consequences whatsoever for humanity! In effect, the Serpent is saying, 'Think, say and do whatever you like, and it'll be fine'! What is already becoming clear is the fact that the Serpent is a liar. We also have the expression today that 'if we hear the same lie repeated again and again, eventually people begin to believe that it's true!'

The Serpent's tactic is subtle but very profound, as he seeks to get into Eve's mind and take control over it. Yes, this woman was attracted to the sight of the apple, but the deeper attraction was surely in the direction of gaining further knowledge that would offer the possibility of becoming like God Himself! "When you eat of it your eyes will be opened, and you will be like God". Yes, it happened a long time ago, but it surely lies at the root of the human desire to be 'like God', whether in the field of technology, job promotion, political ambition, sophisticated weapons of warfare, nuclear arsenals and environmental destruction. The Serpent was seeking to break into the woman's inner world of thought, desire and will, and to captivate all three for his own purposes. The Serpent grabbed all three, as Eve submitted to the temptation and in doing so became trapped in her disobedience to God. Satan, through this subtle disguise, achieved his purpose and plan. At this point, the woman had passed the rubicon, the point of no return and the point at which 'temptation' could with justification be called 'sin' in the divine vocabulary. To put this another way, the long history of Spiritual Warfare had just notched up its first and major battle loss!

The results of the woman's catastrophic decision can be briefly noted, but their consequences are actually vast and widespread, right to the present day. The woman dragged Adam into the battle of ruptured and destructive relationships that ensued, when one person's sin affects and involves others. The two of them felt physically ashamed in their exposure. It's the same sense of defilement when we cheat someone or take unfair advantage of them or unfairly criticize another person. The man and woman hid themselves from the divine presence, as they heard the Lord God walking in the Garden. Sin has estranged humanity from God and when we fall into disobedience, that very disobedience produces distance and God feels a million miles away from us. We have crushed our closeness with God and this is a catastrophic loss to us. Another result of this gaining of new, but forbidden, knowledge was a strange, unexpected and ironic one, namely fear in the man (Genesis 3:10)! Fear affects the human body and tortures the human mind and is the result of sin. How does this work? When human beings walk closely with their God, the relationship is one of love, but when that link is shattered, the love is replaced with fear as a result of the sin. Fear, stress and anxiety are the 'trinity' that drive many lives in the 21st Century across the globe.

Very interestingly, but tragically, in today's world people find it very difficult to say and mean, 'I was wrong'. Sin is covered up today, as it was in the Garden, and the 'blame game' kicks in almost immediately. The man said, "*She* gave me some fruit from the tree and I ate it." He also tries to drag God into the blame: "the woman you put here with me…." The man blames anyone except himself! Eve is just as guilty of this passing the buck (Gen 3:13). We love to blame God for the state of the world that has actually been so messed up by human beings! The massive consequence of all this was that humanity's fellowship with God had been severed and the result was spiritual death. Ever since that moment, though humanity lived and breathed, nevertheless all people were cut off from true spiritual life, and the underlying sin of humanity brought – and guaranteed – divine judgment. God cannot be blamed for this, because the man and woman had actually condemned themselves by their own thoughts, words and actions in the Garden. God could not be deemed unfair in any sense whatsoever. The most unexpected and certainly undeserved consequence of all is the stunning act of God then recorded in Gen 3:21 when God makes skins for the couple and clothes them. That is the generosity and graciousness of God. Ultimately of course God's supreme plan would be to clothe His own people firmly and finally by justifying them with the eternal covering of the righteousness of the Lord Jesus Christ.

MORE BIBLICAL ROOTS OF SATANIC ACTIVITY

Ezekiel – A certain degree of caution needs to be exercised with the material in Ezekiel when it comes to assessing possible clues to the biblical roots of Satan. There is poetic language used here, but in Ezekiel 26-28 the prophet has been engaged in portraying the doom of the kingdom of Tyre, North West of Israel. It belonged to Phoenicia and was an area of great wealth and power. This kingdom had exhibited considerable pride and arrogance. Ezek 28:1-10 deals with the prince of Tyre, referring to a man, while Ezek 28:11-19 refer to the king of Tyre in a lamentation that treats the king in language that could not be considered as suitable for a human being. Both prince and king operate against the living God! The King of Tyre is described as having been in Eden, the Garden of God but having been filled with violence and sinfulness – see Ezek 28:1-10. Similarly the Prince is depicted as having had a proud heart and having claimed to be a god – see Ezek 28:1-10. They were both under divine judgment! The King had been perfect in so many ways and was indeed a created being, but tragically fell and was cast out. Why? Because sin was found in him and he was guilty of being corrupt, violent and proud. He finally was cast out and brought others down with him in that great fall. This whole chapter has remarkable similarities to the Gen 3 truths.

Isaiah – The prophet here is showing a taunt that will be used against the proud and strong king of Babylon in Isaiah 14:10f. This king will be brought down and Isaiah continues to address this issue, but in fact there is a greater figure behind the king of Babylon. Yes, Tyre and Babylon are worldly powers that are in opposition to God, but they are also symbols of a very real demonic power working behind these earthly kings. Babylon is described as having fallen from heaven and as having claimed to be ascending to heaven. These are words that are not really being addressed to a mere human being. These are words from Satan but they are given a response from God Himself that Satan will certainly be brought low. The root issue is that Satan was not happy with his status and in his great pride, he wanted to rise up to attain the status of God Himself. Early scholars believe that Jesus' words regarding Satan's fall from heaven were rooted firmly in Isa 14:12. For example, Jude wrote about "the angels which did not keep their own position but abandoned their proper dwelling" (Jude 6) and Paul wrote to Timothy not to push forward a new convert "or he may be puffed up with conceit and fall into the condemnation of the devil", meaning the condemnation proclaimed on the devil. Satan has always, ever since his fall, pressed men and women in the direction of pride. Humanity was created by God to develop fellowship and dependence on the Lord God.

Gospels – In Luke 10:18 Jesus proclaimed, "I saw Satan fall like lightning from heaven." The intended meaning of these very few words has been debated by scholars for centuries. The setting and context of these words was Jesus' sending out of the seventy. They return rejoicing because demons were subject to them and to the authority of the name of Jesus. These seventy were told that they should rejoice in having had their names written in heaven. A literal understanding *might* be that Jesus had somehow seen that fall take place or that the fall was a still-future event stated as if it had already taken place or that Jesus suddenly saw this vision when the seventy arrived back. The lesson we need to hold onto is the reality of spiritual warfare, the dwelling of Satan in heaven and the glorious fact that Christian believers are assured of heaven and that we do have power in warfare over Satan and his demons.

Book of Revelation - A key text here is certainly Rev 12:7 – "Now war arose in heaven, Michael and his angels fighting against the dragon: and the dragon and his angels fought, but they were defeated and there was no longer any place for them in heaven. And the great dragon was thrown down, that ancient serpent, who is called the Devil and Satan, the deceiver of the whole world, he was thrown down to the earth and his angels were thrown down with him". The primary context of Revelation lies in the first century AD persecution of Christians by the Roman State. Rev 12 clarifies the fact that Satan, an angelic spirit, was an inhabitant of Heaven who rebelled against the Godhead. Michael and his forces succeeded in ousting Satan from Heaven and casting him, together with a third of the stars/angels in Heaven, down to the earth (12:4). This dragon – Satan – now operates in the earthly arena, along with his two key accomplices – the beast from the sea and the beast from the earth. Satan had fallen from his original position as one of God's angels to continue his work of inflicting maximum damage to Christian people and churches.

The Key Features of Satan in Scripture

Scripture affirms a range of Satan's character elements –

He is *strong* – Satan works in human minds to instil fears and doubts; in human bodies he inflicts disease and death; in human spirits to generate immoral desires and proud thoughts. He seeks to infiltrate human organisations, nations, nature (Mk 4:39), crowds of people (John 8:59). Yet, he quakes at the name of Jesus Himself and in reality, he will run scared if God's people firmly resist him in Jesus' powerful name (James 4:7).

He is *vicious* – Satan has already shown this in the Revelation and Ezekiel passages and he can make possessed people very powerful (Mk 5:3). Anger and power are visible in individuals but also in nations that are brazenly atheistic in outlook, attitudes and actions.

He can *dictate* – He is described in Rev 2:13 as having a 'throne' in Pergamum and people living there were required to acknowledge Caesar as sole and sovereign Lord. Satan dictated the ways that economic, political and religious life was corrupted and thus compromised. Some were entering into the "deep things of Satan, as they call them" (Rev 2:24).

He can *possess* people – Satan was sinfully determined to enter the life of Judas Iscariot, with the aim of betraying Jesus, and the Gospel writers record this entry in Lk 22:3 and John 13:27. The devil can take over control of a person's life, becoming master of the house.

He is an inveterate *liar* – Millions of people have believed the lie that Satan does not actually exist and have believed the lie that true freedom can be found in our freedom to think and live in whatever way we choose and enjoy. The actual result of course leads to death. He mimics God and can imitate God's power by offering healing that can bring a person into lifelong bondage to the powers of deep darkness. He works in churches through false teaching and false brethren (1 Tim 1:1-7). He subtly twists truth and perverts doctrine.

He is *capable* – He deceived in the Garden of Eden and tried to deceive Jesus in the wilderness. He is capable of thinking, planning and executing his deceptions. Paul underlines Satan's capability by showing the necessity for all believers to put on 'the whole armour of God' (Eph 6), that we will soon need to consider in our studies.

He *does not give up* – Satan went for Jesus at every opportunity to try to deflect Him, whether immediately after His birth, whether during his arrest and trials or whether His intense weakness on the Cross when he was mocked and insulted (Mk 15:30). He hates the perseverance of suffering and persecuted Christians, as Revelation brings out very clearly.

Satan actually is *restricted and limited* – Satan was judged at the Cross of Calvary. It is surely in the period of the Church Age, between the birth of the Christ and His final Return, that Satan is bound and his power is lessened. Yes, he can hinder the work of God's Kingdom but he certainly cannot prevent it. Satan and his helpers are actually in chains (Rev 20:2; Jude 6). While it is true that we must not see Satan behind every bush in life, yet we must not slip into the danger of underestimating him!

Spiritual Warfare and …
4 …Satan's Tactical Operations in the World

A. The Reality of Enemy Tactics

Following our study of Genesis Chapter 3 and its account of Satan's enticement for humanity to follow his own example of rebellion against God, we now need to ask the question –

What then are Satan's actual goals in this world, following from his fall out of heaven?

The first thing to be clear about is that Satan, in his pride, arrogance and self-delusion, is absolutely fixed on his hatred of the Godhead. Satan actually betrays himself in this regard in the recorded temptations of Jesus in the wilderness, as recorded in Luke 4:1-13; Matt 4:1-11. In these texts, we see the evidence for Satan trying to split the Godhead, driving a wedge between Father and Son by using the weapons of doubt, disobedience and sheer disloyalty. The Enemy is here seeking to discredit and damage the Godhead.

If Satan cannot grab the status and being of God Himself, then he uses a myriad of ways in which to ruin the creation of God, namely the cosmos/universe/world itself. Revelation Chapter 5 clearly establishes that Christ, as slain Lamb of God, alone has the right to break the seals of the scroll of God re human future and God's plan for history. The breaking of the seals opens the way for history to unravel the mess that Satan, in his fallen state, seeks to inflict across God's created world. For example, in Revelation Chapter 6, these seals take the form of the rise of successive military powers; violence between men and groups of men; famines and rising commodity prices, such that the rich grow safely and comfortably richer while the poor struggle to find the next meal; death by disease and by starvation; persecution of Christians that adds to all their other accumulated woes; natural disasters, climatic catastrophes and tectonic events of frightening proportions. Such events are frequently repeated throughout history in varying forms but of increasing intensity. These are warning judgments from God, but in Rev 9:20 the message is that people by and large refuse to listen to God's love. God is hugely patient in waiting for people to heed the warnings and turn to Him in repentance, but human hearts are highly resistant and in this process, Satan inflicts great damage on God's created world.

Not only does Satan target the world, he aims his poisonous assaults especially against those who are seeking to live as serious disciples of the Lord Jesus Christ. Scripture confirms this very clearly in Revelation 12 by the image of the dragon, Satan, warring against "the seed of the woman, those who keep the commandments of God and bear testimony to Jesus". Again in Rev 17:3 we see the image of the harlot – of Babylon/Rome – "Babylon the great, mother of harlots and of earth's abominations. And I saw the woman, drunk with the blood of the saints, and the blood of the martyrs of Jesus". Sometimes the warfare takes the form of open and outright opposition; other times a much more subtle and seductive infiltration of Jesus's followers. How does this work in practice? Satan allows life's pressures to invade our lives, but his purpose is that we should be *overwhelmed* by them. God, on the other hand, allows pain, struggle and pressure into our lives, but His purpose is that we *overcome* and are matured/strengthened. We need to remember that temptation itself *is not sin*, but it becomes sin if we yield to the temptation. It's a familiar downward spiral that progresses like this – thoughts solidify into word, and word becomes deed, and deed becomes habit, and habit becomes character and character traps us into our final state in life .and death. See the connected string of texts in James 1:13-14; Heb 4:15; 2 Pet 2:19. Jesus Himself endured temptation repeatedly but without giving in.

What then are Satan's actual reasons and strategies in warfare?

The Key Issue – Why is Satan so constantly looking to pull humanity into a downward direction? Satan was created a wonderful creature of immense power. He had been greatly gifted by God but Satan treated these gifts as a means to exercising great power. Rather than expressing gratitude to God, Satan refused to acknowledge God as the Lord of his life, but instead the evil one longed to replace God and to receive worship to himself from a deceived humanity across the globe. Crucial in Satan's strategy is his universal success in "blinding the minds of the unbelievers to keep them from seeing the light of the gospel of the glory of Christ, who is the likeness of God" (2 Cor. 4:3ff). What the Apostle Paul is saying is simply but truthfully that gospel proclamation is tough work that requires persistent energy, determination, godliness and great courage because this work hits the barrier of fierce Satanic opposition wherever it is practised. Satan resents losing his prisoners into the Kingdom of Christ, for essentially he has taken God's place in many lives and he asserts all his energy to keep unbelievers in the bondage of their unbelief. His top priority is to prevent the light of Christ's gospel breaking into dark lives. Thus he imparts 'blindness' into the minds of unbelievers and though they may not be evil people, nevertheless they are spiritually blinded! Luke 8:12 and Matt 13:37ff record the Parable of the Sower and noted that the devil steals the Word of the Gospel from their minds and hearts. Whenever a person does respond to this glorious Word of Life, Satan springs into activity to try to crush and obliterate the new spiritual life that a convert has. For as long as a person is happy and settled in Satan's realm, though actually unconscious of it, then Satan won't trouble that person too much. But if that person dare cross the boundary into the life and territory of Jesus, then Satan will hurl all he possibly can at that person to try to drag him or her down.

Satan's use of cynicism and doubt – He will expend huge energy to pour scorn on the truth of Scripture, using unbelievers who are claiming the presence of multiple 'mistakes' in the Bible and the various Bible versions that differ from each other, leaving seekers in a muddle of confusion, doubt and disbelief, not to mention those 'universalists' who teach that all religions lead to the same Christ!

Satan's gagging of Christian believers – The silence of God's people regarding their own life-saving and life-changing faith in Christ, is guaranteed to keep unbelievers firmly trapped in the Kingdom of Satan. Some Christians are fearful of explaining the gospel, while others argue that it's your life that counts, not your spoken words! Some feel that faith needs to be kept private, rather than be 'aired' in public. Some even assert that kind atheists really don't need the gospel at all. The gospel *does need* to be *spoken*, as well as lived out, in every arena where people will listen to it!

Satan splinters churches into states of disunity – Satan will find his way into churches and will raise up differences within and between denominations. A church that is divided cannot seriously expect evangelism to preach a gospel of reconciliation! Social class and endemic gossip in a church form a double dose of toxicity that will paralyze the impact and credibility of the gospel. Read the Letter of James in the New Testament.

Satan creates disharmony – It remains the case today that Satan will search out relationships, partnerships and marriages where one of the persons is a spiritually weak link that may well cause a breakdown of the union, even if it happens very slowly. Often it will be the Christian partner who gradually compromises, as Satan works insidiously and covertly to weaken the spiritual bonds of both partners within the union.

Satan exerts pressures of all sorts – Satan will seek to keep people away from Christ if they sense that conversion to Christ could lead to trouble, be it persecution, financial loss, social stigma or family embarrassment. Living faith could restrict our job opportunities, access to medical help, poverty, discrimination, martyrdom, exclusion from our friends, family and futures. Satan is absolutely delighted, though sometimes of course, he loses out, if Christian suffering triggers displays of unbelievers' compassion or if governments unexpectedly step in to defend and protect believers. Above all, Satan wants people to acknowledge *his power* and he longs to prevent men and women from declaring their allegiance to his conqueror, the Christ. When people change sides and truly embrace Christ, Satan will use every possible weapon at his disposal to pull them back to the side of evil, or failing that, to destroy their new faith.

B. The Realisation of Enemy Tactics

What then are Satan's methods and tactics of warfare?

An A-Z OF DEMONIC INTERFERENCE

Activity
a) Satan ***Exercises*** sway and control over the entire world – 1 John 5:19;
b) Satan ***Employs*** power to hold people in a condition and state of spiritual darkness – Acts 26:15-18; 2 Cor 4:4;
c) Satan ***Encourages*** people to live out their lives by following the ways of this fallen and corrupted world. This takes the form of living in a state of sin and disobedience, two concepts that Satan successfully shoves into oblivion in the vocabulary and understanding of contemporary society – Eph 2:1-3.

Affliction – Satan seeks and grabs opportunities to afflict God's people

a) by *Depression* and *Discouragement* through his accusations. Thus for example, in Zechariah 3:1ff, the high priest **Joshua** stood before the angel of the Lord, with Satan standing at his right side to accuse him. The Lord says to Satan "The Lord rebuke you, Satan! The Lord, who has chosen Jerusalem, rebuke you! Is not this man a burning stick snatched from the fire?" The angel forgives Joshua for his sin, by removing his dirty clothes and promises cleansing for the land if Joshua and those following him will walk in obedience to the Lord. We can identify other cases such as that in 1 Samuel 18 which records how an "evil spirit from the Lord troubled **Saul** and turned him not merely into a depressive but a manic depressive" (18:1).

Elijah, having won a great victory over the prophets of Baal, retired into the wilderness in deep and dark depression, feeling that the cause of God was lost and that only he was left (1 Kings 18). We do need to be careful here however, because not all depression or discouragement is demonic. However, *some* depression is caused by demonic attacks and if that is the cause, then it will respond to prayer in Jesus' name. We must remember that we will be very vulnerable to Satan's assaults after periods of rich fellowship and fruitful ministry!

b) by *Direct Attack* – Job 1:13-19; 2:7-10; John 8:44; Luke 13:10-17; Acts 10:38. Again, we must not connect all disease or suffering to direct, demonic activity. Satan works in the form of attack, but he then seeks follow-up in the way we ourselves respond to his attacks through *fear, discouragement or stress.* This is a very common tactic!

c) by *Division And Disunity* – See Titus for examples. Satan will divide and disunite by his attacks amongst families, churches, Christian workers, missionaries, Christian organizations and Bible/Theological teachers and students.

Deception – Satan's ability to lie, tell half-truths or bend truth is virtually without limit. Consider this wide range of biblical examples

a) Satan creates various diversions from devotion – 2 Cor 11:1-5;

b) Satan operates with huge subtlety as an angel of light, especially in the area of defective Christology that infects most sects and cultic teachings – 2 Cor 11:12-15;

c) Satan specialises in counterfeit, even including signs and miracles – Matt 24:24; 1 Tim 4:1-2;

d) Satan deceives people about their standing before God – John 8:39-43;

e) Satan was, is and always will be, totally committed to lies: John 8:44-47;

f) Satan is utterly devoid of truth – John 8:44;

g) Satan's hatred of the life-giving power of truth is reflected in the Jews' hatred of Jesus – John 8:51,52,59;

h) Satan seeks to deny all that we have been made in Christ, all that we now have and are in Christ, and all that we will be in Christ;

i) Satan works constantly to project a false view of God – Genesis 3;

j) Satan cannot believe that God is love, that He loves His people or that human recipients of that love can truly love God in return – Job 1-2.

Desire – Here we actually have two issues working in opposite directions. Illicit sexual desire, otherwise known as 'lust', invades our lives from a whole range of media, advertising and cheap literature. No one is exempt from such temptation, regardless of status and degree of life experience. Images torment the mind and there are only a few short steps into pondering, weighing up the consequences and decisions to act in disobedience to God. A whole range of sins is rapidly opened up for our actual involvement. The tale of David and Bathsheba is well known and translates into many contemporary settings today. This chain of events is a profound favourite in Satan's armoury of fatal temptations. Alongside this weapon, Satan is subtle enough to swing to the polar opposite extreme and to create situations where we take on board forms of abstinence or asceticism that Paul condemns as 'giving heed to demonic doctrines' (1 Tim 4:3). Such sins are liable to be indulged in by those who have taken vows of celibacy, an abstention from marriage which puts its participants in severe and serious risk of committing 'survival sins' that actually trigger immoral relationships as a way of gaining temporary escape from the mental and physical torture of 'alternatives' to celibacy. In short, we can conclude that dealing with temptation can take us to two possible unhealthy extremes of the spectrum – either towards over-indulgence or towards false asceticism.

The crucial antidote to such temptations is the believer's calling and responsibility to shed the clothing of the 'old nature' of pre-Christian living, listed by the Apostle Paul in Ephesians 4:22ff, namely idolatry, lies, anger, theft, moods, malice, laziness, dirty conversations, bitterness, fornication and bad temper. Colossians 3:5ff repeats much of this evil mix, as does Peter in his First Letter 2:1ff. The cluster of temptations to these and other sins are also highlighted in James 1:21 and Romans 13:12. In short, the NT writers are united in all that is to be shunned and ruthlessly avoided by Christian disciples in the life of Spiritual Warfare, that absolutely demands our constant use of prayer and the power of Christ and His Spirit to counter the assaults of Satan, who is so subtle in his timings and methods, so attracting in his suggestions and so determined to trip us up, with catastrophic consequences for our lives, families and churches.

Disaster – We can so easily fall into temptation by sudden or unexpected changes in our life's circumstances, especially if such changes hurl us into deep uncertainty or dark unpredictability about the future! This can be rooted in local, national, global or personal disasters or by physical misfortunes. Satan orchestrated that toxic cocktail in Job's life and circumstances. He lost animals and property, was bereaved, was profoundly unwell, and yet in all this, God was still in control! Again we need to beware of claiming that *every* piece of bad luck, *every* sickness, *every* misfortune is brought by the devil! *Sometimes* it is demonic: this was Paul's experience in 2 Cor 12:7ff with his 'thorn in the flesh'. Paul prayed for this 'thorn' to be removed, but to no avail. Nevertheless Paul did receive special grace from God to handle this huge challenge to his life and ministry.

Doubts – Satan was and is very familiar with this tactic of his! He tempted Eve with that question, "Did God say…?" He tempted Jesus, "if you are the Son of God…" Many Christians are unsure of their standing with God and their acceptance by Him. Jesus never forgot this challenge from Simon Peter after his great confession of faith at Caesarea Philippi. God had spoken through Peter, but then immediately Satan spoke through him in Matt 16:16f; Mark 8:32f. This was a subtle attack of doubt but the Lord saw it straight away and rebuked Peter, saying "Get behind me, Satan!" (Mark 8:33). That was, and still is, precisely how to handle doubts that Satan drops on top of us. Satan does not know how to respond to the massive power of Scripture, Prayer and the power of the Holy Spirit we possess.

Fear – This is a very common and very effective weapon in the hands of Satan. He employs it very frequently indeed in our lives and ministries. Satan was sifting Peter just like grain on that night of Jesus' arrest. The impact on Peter was so heavy that he lacked the courage even to admit to a maidservant about his allegiance to Jesus (Luke 22:31ff). 'Satan' and 'fear' are basically joined at the hip. They are inseparable. Many of us are terrified to admit to friends, families, colleagues that we belong to Christ. The Enemy encourages such silence. It is also very true that when our lives and circumstances are suddenly rocked by disasters, illness, financial downturn or a bad medical prognosis, the circumstance itself is not necessarily the main issue, but rather the terrors and fears that build up in our minds, hearts and emotions. Satan loves to pour petrol on these fears that have set fire to our fragile minds and emotions. Even a relatively small fire is then easily fanned by Satan into a raging inferno that may turn out to be far bigger that the actual reality of the problem itself.

Fiery Arrows – Paul in Ephesians 6 warns us that Satan has a very large quiver full of poisonous arrows that will create maximum damage to the Christian cause and in a very wide variety of ways! Virtually all of Satan's firing of fiery arrows can be found through this particular Sermon Four. In the broadest sense, Satan loves to stop men and women from keeping, defending and practising Jesus's two great commandments, namely to love God and to love neighbour. He loves to see believers break these two massive commands. How many of us have truly put God first? How often have we failed to grasp the reality of God or taken his name in vain or neglected/disrespected our own parents? How often have we murdered by thought, word or look? How often have we committed adultery in desire or fact? What about covetousness in our materialistic Western world? Satan pulls us down in these very areas.

We now need to conclude with three major features of Satan's warfare against the believer, the church and the leaders of the church.

Pride – Satan himself crashed to earth to continue and intensify his work, simply because of his disastrous fall from the grace of God. A severe warning is issued to us by Paul in 1 Cor 10:12, "Let anyone who thinks that he stands take heed lest he fall". Pride was the greatest of Satan's own sin, so he readily passes this on to us as the master of pride. It was pride that paralyzed many Pharisees into a failure to find justification in Christ alone (Luke 18:11). God resists and resents those who are proud (1 Peter 5:5,8). John Wesley astutely said in his book *The Devil* "Pride is a strange illness – it makes everyone sick but the one who has it"!

Slander – Satan conducts a continual smear-campaign against God, see Job 1:9-11; 2:4-5; Rev 12:10-11. He expresses this accusation against God by accusing Christ and His Church. The result of this is the presence of suspicion, mistrust, pride and division within the churches of God. Satan reflects these features of his own nature *through* people, *including believers!* Check out Galatians 5:19-21.

Temptation – Now we come as it were full circle back to the future, as well as to the past and present! We recall the crucial importance of texts such as Gen 3; Matt 4:1-11; Eph 4:27; 6:11; James 1:13-18; 1 John 2:12-29. What are Satan's methods in this drive to tempt us all?

a) To divert us from *believing God's Word.* As we have noted already, Satan blinds the eyes of unbelievers and closes them to the truth of Christ's Gospel – 2 Cor 4:4; 2 Tim 2:26.

b) To divert us from *obeying God's Will* – John 6:70; 2 Tim 4:3-5; 1 Pet 5:8

c) To divert us from *walking in God's Way* – 2 Peter 3:17-18; Jude 4.

Spiritual Warfare and …

5 …the Form of Satanic assaults on ministers *et al.*

including church members, leaders and missionaries.

A. Typical Satanic tactics aimed against Ministers

In a brief web article – *Pastoral Ministry and Spiritual Warfare* – Nicholas T. Batzig expresses deep regret over the passing of the Puritan era, with its strong awareness of the fact that "Pastoral ministry is unrelenting spiritual warfare"…. "Sadly, with few exceptions, the Reformed church in our day has largely dismissed this massively important element of the Christian life"…. "The worst thing that the church can do is to let her guard down. Both ministers and congregants alike must recognise that this is the case." Texts such as 1 Thess 2:18 and 2 Tim 4:17 show just how aware the Apostle Paul was of the huge arena of spiritual warfare in which he was constantly engaged! Let's consider briefly a few points made by Batzig, who concludes, "What congregations and ministers need more than almost anything else today is a robust understanding of spiritual warfare".

So how does Satan exercise his venomous strategies against ministers of the Gospel of the Lord Jesus Christ?

Temptation to Pride – We've already noted that Paul was not happy with a person becoming an elder, if that person is new to the faith and therfore at risk of pride and a fall *into the same condemnation as the devil* (1 Tim 3:6). This serious risk of falling through pride is never far away from us. The triple antidote seems to be humility, maturity and suffering, harsh and hard as that may sound! Age, wisdom and popularity are of course by no means guaranteed protection against falling. Paul believed that his own gifts required the testing and hard knocking of his "thorn in the side…. lest he be raised above measure" (2 Cor 12:7). We absolutely need to guard ourselves in our minds, hearts and wills against this Satanic grenade!

Temptation to Discouragement – That fatal mix of triple strategies of divisions, setbacks and complainants in our churches is a very common source of discouragement. Discouragement is a very common cocktail of a range of subtle factors. Sometimes the source is Satan's interference in the very circumstances of our lives. Paul was convinced that Satan had hindered him from coming to the Thessalonians (1 Thess 2:18). Satan can spoil our plans and 'throw spanners in the way' and follow this up very quickly by assaulting our minds in ways that accelerate and escalate – we feel disappointed in wrecked plans; we blame ourselves for it; "if I were a better minister, these setbacks would not be happening". Satan draws close and whispers in our ears, "not seeing much fruit are you? Maybe you're past your sell-by date? Maybe there are more gifted members that could replace you? Are you actually working hard enough? You could have a much easier life elsewhere, you know?"

One series of triple helps for us can be found in the sequence 2 Cor 2:13; 2 Tim 4:16; 2 Tim 4:17! This is an antidote to spiritual paralysis. Sometimes it's simply, but significantly, one difficult person or one awkward family in the church who are used by the Enemy to sow seeds of discord and division across the church. It was just the one – the one disciple who betrayed Jesus, once Satan had invaded that life of Judas (Matt 26:14-15) and all for the sake of 30 pieces of silver (John 13:27). How often do we fail, in the heat of the battle, to realise the true source of evil attacks?

Temptation to Fear – Fear works in all sorts of directions and deceptions. For example, Paul warns Timothy of the challenges and difficulties he will face in his gospel ministry and urges him to be courageous and fearless in carrying out this work – see 2 Tim 1:6-14. Timothy was fearful of other people. The Apostle Paul frequently brings Timothy back to the necessity for vigilance and awareness of being in the midst of an unrelenting spiritual battle. In his great fear, when he cowered outside the High Priest's house, Peter crumbled and collapsed, to the point of denying his allegiance to Jesus, and even his mere presence with Jesus (Luke 22:54-62). One of the strongest biblical reminders to us all is that the Lord God Almighty, in the Trinity of the Godhead, has actually called us into the ministry of the Gospel (1 Tim 1:18; 2 Tim 2:1-7). We need to remind Satan of these deeply profound and personal Scriptures.

The experience of many of us is that one of Satan's chief weapons is to work on our minds and emotions in such a way that virtually our only focus is our concentration on our own fears. Satan's trick is to hide himself but work like mad to exaggerate and emphasise the negatives of our circumstances, so that we are paralyzed by fears that are ungrounded in reality but instead, blown up out of all proportion to the reality of the situation. Yes, Satan *can afflict* the people of God in tangible ways but his main direction of attack is to engender a debilitating and disheartening sense of fear. We wait for the biopsy results, convinced of the worst possible outcome. Satan loves to play on our fears of the uncertainty, unease, and unpredictability of our health, futures, finances and fitness. He hates the idea of our resting in the love, provision, direction and assurance of the living Almighty God Himself. He works to unsettle us.

Temptation to Deviate from the Gospel – The life, death, resurrection, ascension and reign of Christ lie at the very heart of the Christian Gospel. When Peter recoiled from the very thought that Jesus would be killed, the response of the Lord was brutally direct and uncompromising – "Get behind me, Satan" – as Jesus rebuked Peter. Satan desired to suggest to Peter that there was surely an easier path and an easier message than that of crucifixion. Satan today seeks to persuade ministers that there must be an easier, more convincing and more conducive route to the forgiveness of sin and the gift of eternal life. We need to persevere in our faithfulness to the Gospel of Christ, preaching that 'crazy' gospel of Paul's, "for the message of the cross is foolishness to those who are perishing, but to us who are being saved it is the power of God" (1 Corinthians 1:18-2:5). Such communication of gospel truth will engage us in spiritual warfare and we must never fail to be aware of that. Yes, the Lord Jesus Christ is utterly victorious over Satan and all his powers of demonic darkness. At the same time though, we need to be very conscious of our own weakness, frailty and sinfulness. Crucially, as well, we need to be aware of the Enemy's strategies, watching out for them and constantly praying against such demonic tactics of warfare. As ministers, we need regularly to remind our people that all sincere and serious disciples will come under relentless attack from the living and active powers and principalities.

B. Specific Satanic attacks aimed at the Apostle Paul
His understanding and experience of spiritual warfare in his second letter to the Corinthians

Martyn Lloyd Jones was totally convinced about the reality of Spiritual Warfare. He wrote in one of his many books "The first thing we have to realise is that the Christian life is a *warfare,* that we are strangers in an alien land, that we are in the enemy's territory.... The teaching which gives the impression that the pathway to glory is all easy and simple and smooth is not Christianity". The Apostle Paul was also completely certain about the truth and challenge to Christians posed by Spiritual Warfare. The evidence of my enquiries into Paul's own engagement in Spiritual Warfare in 2 Corinthians seems to indicate that Paul was more willing to *write* about his experiences more freely than many churches are willing to *recognise* even the existence of such warfare.

Let's trawl through the text of 2 Corinthians to search out actual evidence of the hidden, but tangible, work of Satan and his armies.

Let's look at this under the headings:
Problem Manifested, Enemy Strategy, Weapons & Resources, Outcomes.

CH 1 ***Problem Manifested:*** The whole content and atmosphere of this chapter revolves around the issue of the interplay between suffering and comfort, alongside the sovereign intervention of God Himself. Pauline teaching elsewhere in 2 Cor and in other letters indicates that such struggles in ministry are indeed connected with spiritual warfare, even where Satan and his demonic forces are not specifically named.

Enemy Strategy: Paul reports extensive experience of troubles (1:4), sufferings (1:5,6,7), distress (1:6), hardships (1:8), great pressure (1:8), despair of life (1:8), the emotional feel of a death sentence upon his very life and ministry (1:9).

Weapons/Resources: The apostle recalls that he actually belongs to Christ as his apostle and that this is according to the will of God. This strengthens Paul's sense of assurance of the presence and power of the Lord in the midst of battle. He likewise finds encouragement from the knowledge of the reality of grace and peace of the Godhead that are his and the Corinthian believers' for the warfare of life and ministry. He finds help to be able to reflect on the ***character*** of God – His compassion and comfort – and that in itself causes him to overflow in praise and worship, even in the midst of trouble when times are very tough. Our comfort from God then overflows into the lives of others who are also struggling in warfare (1:5) and this yields patient endurance in the church, even in pain. Indeed the church shares in the sufferings and comfort of Christ and His workers, and the positive result is that Paul has confident hope for this church (1:7). Paul does not hide the severity of his hardships in Asia (1:8-11). The battles were unrelenting, yet all this was to force Paul and his team to cast themselves firmly on the God who raised Christ from the dead (1:9). That is how powerful God is to intervene in our lives.

Outcomes: The result of all this was sixfold –

a) It cured Paul and his fellow-workers from the perils of self-reliance in Christian life and ministry, instead of total dependence on the Lord Himself (1:9).

b) Paul's struggles became a platform for the display of God's ability to deliver His workers, not only in the past and present, but in the future as well.

c) Such dilemmas and distresses in ministry had brought forth a volume of prayer that was fruitful in helping those in the heat of warfare and triggered an avalanche of gratitude for God's response to prayer (1:11).

d) It should also be noted that one of Paul's chief weapons in the warfare against the powers of darkness was his relational lifestyle of holiness and sincerity that came from God (1:12-13). Paul and his co-workers lived godly lives in the Church *and* in the world of such quality and of such rootedness in the grace of God, that their level of living confounded both their human and demonic opponents.

e) Indeed their attitudes and actions, plus their clear writing to the church, produced increasingly positive relational understanding of the sort that makes it so much harder for Satan and his demons to confuse and deflect church relationships – one of his prime methods of screwing up and destroying inter-personal relationships within the church's life. Both Paul and his co-workers *and* the Corinthian Church will boast of each other and be proud of each other, when Christ returns and we all stand before His Judgment Seat to give an account of our lives and ministries.

f) With reference to his travel plans to visit the Corinthians, Paul speaks of his spiritual, not worldly, way of planning his itinerary (1:15-17). We are to be positive in our planning, speaking and actions, just as God makes His promises that are always 'Yes' in Christ Jesus. We are to be true and faithful in all we are and do and that stance will be a key part of our weaponry in spiritual warfare because as we live trustworthy lives in this world, so God will make the church stand firm in Christ, will be glorified in this firmness, will anoint us, will assure us by setting His seal of ownership on us, will put His Spirit within us as a deposit of a future guarantee of eternity and will grant us the gift of joy to stand firm in faith (1:18-24). This is how God strengthens us in the middle of the spiritual battles that we fight. Paul's decision not to return to Corinth was rooted in love and mercy!

<u>CH 2</u> ***Problem Manifested:*** Instead of making a painful visit to the Corinthians and ending up distressed by what was going on in the church, Paul writes a very painful letter to them instead. A visit would have upset him because he would have met up with those who ought to have made him rejoice, but instead were continuing to live in a state of sin. The bottom line was that the Apostle Paul loved his churches deeply and wanted to see them growing to spiritual completion and maturity – see Col 1:24-2:5. It is possible that Paul is referring here to the incestuous brother dealt with in 1 Cor 5:1-5 which interestingly also mentions 'handing this man over to Satan' (v.5). It could however refer to the unnamed individual who had sought to attack, criticise and undermine Paul very publicly during his last visit to Corinth and had been the trigger for Paul's severe letter mentioned

in 2:3-4. Paul clearly had many critics in the Corinthian church who were questioning and critiquing his apostolic authority. The apostle urges the Corinthians not to go to extremes in their discipline of this forgiven offender. Rather the church ought to forgive, comfort and love the offender. The verb used by Paul in 2:5 – 'he has grieved all of you' – is in the Perfect Tense and suggests there is an on-going sense of tension, unsettledness and grief in the Corinthian Christian community. This is potentially dangerous. Paul *had* been hurt, along with the community, but he responds in forgiveness for the community's sake.

Enemy Strategy: – Paul warns his readers in Corinth that this scenario has the seeds of potential warfare implanted into it. Satan will exploit such a situation for his own disruptive ends, even if the church has already disciplined and forgiven the offender. 'Enough is enough', says Paul in effect! If they are *too severe*, discouragement for the offender and disunity in the church might set in, but if they are *too lenient*, the church will appear to be weak and liberal-minded. Both scenarios are ideal and fertile territory for Satan to play his games over interpersonal relationships – 2:10-11.

Weapons/Resources: Paul is trying to get the Corinthian Community to realise and accept that this difficult person had in fact hurt and damaged the whole community and not just the apostle himself. Paul uses a negative present active subjunctive in a preventative sense. In other words, he is warning them against heaping up too many burdensome words against the offender. The apostle does not want either himself or the church to press the issue any further. He doesn't want to add any additional burdens at this stage. 2:6-7 indicates that the punishment – separation from fellowship – had been imposed by the majority of the community and that it had been sufficient to achieve its intended ends. It was now imperative that warm fellowship be restored to the forgiven offender. The verb *charizomai* means graciously to extend forgiveness. This is a very powerful weapon against Satan in the hands of any Christian community and the goal is not just to give comfort but also to bring deep encouragement. Paul wants the church to make a conscious decision to embrace this person in love. Punishing a person, without the mechanism for healing, is sterile and futile.

Outcomes: Paul explains in 2:9 that he had another motive for writing so strongly to the Corinthians, namely that his instructions about church discipline were intended to test whether the church was serious about obedience to the apostolic authority of Paul. This would show their true character as a church. Paul is aiming for reconciliation and is more than ready to forgive since he has seen this church forgive the offender. Paul is *not* looking for some sort of self-seeking or self-vindicating outcome, but rather whatever will honour Christ and build the church in Corinth. In 2:10 Paul almost plays down the extent of his forgiving stance! This was done 'in the sight of Christ for your sake' – Christ and Church were his prime considerations. Such sacrificial selflessness is a key antidote to the assaults of the Enemy who seeks to split churches all the time. He was trying to diffuse a still-volatile situation and take the hot steam out of it! Satan constantly thinks and schemes to inject and spread disunity throughout the Church. Paul's approach is to encourage the church to stand against this by the exercise of *forgiveness* and *reconciliation.* Powerful weapons indeed! Satan can, however, triumph in such situations in a number of ways – it's true that church discipline expresses grace whilst upholding healthy accountability and protecting a strong church community.

However, there are churches that are so bent on showing 'grace' that they sweep even obvious sin right under the carpet. Sometimes that is because of cultural pressure not to confront people directly or because of immature spirituality or because of a failure to realise that grace is not only about forgiving but about promoting life transformation. Such failure damages a church's witness to the world and keeps a church in bondage. The other side of the coin is the kind of over–zealous discipline that punishes rather than promotes true restoration into community. There are dangers in both directions and Satan looks for opportunities to pursue both weaknesses!

In 2:14-17, Paul writes 'But thanks be to God, who always leads us in triumphal procession in Christ and through us spreads everywhere the fragrance of the knowledge of him'. Paul here is not depicting himself as a victorious Roman general or as a soldier in God's army who has a share in Christ's glorious triumph, but rather as a defeated prisoner who has been put on a humiliating display. Instead of what would seem to be a crushing defeat of God's purposes by Satan and his demons, Paul is actually shown in a life and ministry that reveals the power and the majesty of God in the gospel of Christ, albeit God is actually defeating Satan *through* the suffering, defeat and humiliation of Paul. This of course remarkably parallels the apparent but false victory of Satan in the Calvary Cross! True, before Paul followed Christ, he was an 'enemy of God' (Rom 5:10) and had to be conquered by Christ. Captured prisoners were dragged along to elevate the glory of the triumphant general and ultimately to honour the gods who had won for him the victory. Paul uses this image to show that it is not the Roman Empire or Emperor who is ultimately victorious but rather the God who is fully revealed in the death and resurrection of Jesus Christ. It is God, not Satan, who rules this universe. Paul in his weakness and suffering was challenging the power, success and triumphalism of some of the

Corinthians. Paul argues that his very suffering and weakness in life and ministry actually reveals the power of God. The Lord does not make Christ's followers 'winners' and 'success stories' by the world's standards but He takes them captive and leads them as humiliated, defeated prisoners. Paul however has no regrets. He rejects a life in the service of Satan that would guarantee eternal condemnation and instead embraces fully and wholeheartedly a life as a prisoner and slave of his glorious and victorious God.

In all of this, our calling is not to peddle the word of God for profit, like the false teachers who had infiltrated the Corinthian Church. Rather we are to speak *in Christ, before God* and *with sincerity,* like men sent from God. Herein lies our great weapon of the Word of God, with which we demolish strongholds of Satan, watching God set free the captives from their bondage to Satan – 2:17. It is vital that we never forget that our ministry in and of the Word of God does not consist of mere explanation. It actually is a word either of salvation or of utter devastation, and sends folk either into spiritual life or spiritual death (2:15-16); either into the kingdom of light or the kingdom of eternal darkness under the judgment of God. Our ministries in the Word divide humanity into two destinies and our responsibility is to minister that Word rooted in a life of authenticity and integrity. Our life and ministry are to be a sweet fragrance to God but will take people towards life or death. That is the huge level of responsibility we carry! No wonder the apostle Paul asks the question, 'And who is equal to such a task?' (2:16). Yet, just as Paul has written about the reality that 'in Christ we speak before God with sincerity' (2:17), so he is also hugely confident that by the Spirit's work, the Corinthian Church had come to birth and lives had been changed (3:1-3) for time and eternity. Indeed, Paul is able to write confidently that the Corinthians are a 'letter from Christ', 'the result of our ministry' (3:3). And the basis of his confidence? 'Such confidence as this is ours *through Christ before God* (3:4). In himself Paul – and in ourselves we – have no competence *but 'he has made us competent as ministers of a new Covenant – not of the letter but of the Spirit; for the letter kills, but the Spirit gives life' (3:4-6).*

<u>**CH 3**</u> ***Problem Manifested:*** – The theme of the life-giving New Covenant in Christ by the Spirit is introduced in 2 Cor 3 and the apostle writes of his confidence and competence as a minister of this covenant by God's grace. As he stresses the immense glory of this New Covenant, he returns again to his confidence in this glorious gospel of Christ (3:12). Because of this great hope, Paul concludes that '…we are very bold' (3:12).

Enemy Strategy: Our calling, like Paul's, is to communicate spiritual truth in a world that presents considerable spiritual barriers. We all know the experience of addressing hearts that are actually and really 'veiled' (3:13-18). Paul refers here to the spiritual dullness and blindness that veils human hearts – 3:14 – and has its ultimate cause in demonic deception. Paul's line of argument here starts in 3:7-11. The Spirit was at work in Moses' ministry and Moses did experience the glory of God but the veil on Moses' face effectively separated the people from the glory of God. Therefore, the Israelites did not experience the presence or glory of God through the Spirit. This ministry of the law thus functioned as a 'ministry that brought death' (3:7) and 'condemnation' (3:9). The difference with New Covenant ministry is that it produces 'righteousness' in the human heart, which overflows in great glory (3:9). The New Covenant ministry is not veiled in the way that the Old Covenant was (3:13) and can be preached and taught with great boldness and openness (3:12). *However, the point is this:* hearers of the gospel message in Paul's day still present hardened minds as 'enemies of God' plus veils across their hearts; the result is they fail to understand the message of God ministered by Moses. (3:14-15). Only in Christ, and by the work of His Spirit, can a person experience the removal of the veil that has been covering their heart (3:16) and begin the journey of saving faith that brings continuing transformation of their life in union with Christ (3:18). As Paul explains in detail, especially in Rom. 1:18-25 and in the early chapters of 1 Corinthians, when this veil is removed, the barrier between people and God is smashed apart and all who turn to Christ can then experience the power, presence and glory of God which, prior to that, were utterly impossible for humans to achieve.

Weapons/Resources: Our key weapons in breaking through the spiritual darkness of fallen human nature are the inter-connected weapons that come from God Himself – Word, Christ, Spirit, New Life, Righteousness, Prayer, Faith, Truth, Gospel, Salvation. This is how Paul attacked the false and demonically deceived teachers in Corinth who, whether aware or unaware, were attempting to live and minister 'a different Jesus, a different gospel and a different Spirit' (2 Cor 11:4) in the midst of Corinth's first century AD Celebrity Culture of shallowness, falsity, pretense, ignorance and deception. How little has actually changed since then!

Outcomes: How crucial in our communication, therefore, is
the Spirit's new-covenant enabling in ministry (3:4-6) and
our own transformation of our living by the Spirit of the Lord (3:18).

__CH 4__ ***Problem Manifested:*** The reference to deception, distortion and discouragement ultimately finds their cause in the powers of darkness that seek to deal in such negativity in order to drag down those who seek to serve Christ and the Church actively. Paul's comments in chapter 4 suggest that he and other co-workers have at times been tempted towards despondency and despair in the midst of Christian life and ministry. Paul however again recalls his experiences of real weakness (4:7-12). He has been on the verge of being pressed to breaking point, perplexed, persecuted, struck down, and yet not quite! God has intervened when more grace or deliverance was needed. Indeed, this treasure of the gospel has been placed by God into frail human hands – 'jars of clay' (4:7) – in order 'to show that this all-surpassing power is from God and not from us' (4:7). The following verses show that in spite of constant opposition and attacks, God intervenes and reveals in the Corinthians the life of Christ amidst the dark assaults. It is our enemy who would want us to lose heart – 4:1, 16.

Enemy Strategy: In Romans 9:1-5 and 10:1-4, the Apostle Paul declares his willingness, if it were possible, to lose his salvation, if by that, he might see the salvation of his fellow Jews. That's how desperate Paul is to see people saved. In 1 Cor 9:19-23 he likewise records just how much he longs for the Corinthians to come to a living faith in Christ. How formidable are the obstacles that Satan has put across the road that leads to salvation by belief into Christ! Indeed verse 4 of 2 Cor 4 reveals that it is 'the god of this age who has blinded the minds of unbelievers, so that they cannot see the light of the gospel of the glory of Christ, who is the image of God'.

Weapons/Resources: Paul takes heart amidst all this pressure from the Enemy to subvert the purposes of God for His gospel of Christ in the lives of both Jews and Gentiles. He lists a number of positive encouragements:

a) The apostle rejoices that this ministry has come to us in the purposes and will of God and because of divine mercy (4:1). This in itself is encouraging for it indicates that God is with us in all this!

b) Even the sufferings that Paul is called upon to endure in this life have been ordained by the Lord, in order that in his weakness and pain, it might be blindingly obvious that the power to overturn Satan's work lies in the Godhead, not in the mission or ministry team!

c) Even the pain we struggle with is achieving for us 'an eternal glory that far outweighs it all' (4:17).

The weapons that Paul calls us to employ in this battle are as follows – a) Our life must reflect our rejection of secret and shameful ways – the power of a righteous life is immense (4:2).

b) We are not to deceive people by distorting the Word of God, but rather we are to proclaim and explain it clearly, knowing that the Word will fulfil its purposes in the lives of those who the Spirit will turn to him (4:3).
c) We are to minister in a servant spirit with our focus not on ourselves but in our proclamation of Jesus Christ as Lord (4:5).
d) Remember this – that just as God worked His miracle of grace in *our* lives, so He is able to do the same in the lives of others (4:7).
e) We are called constantly to die with Christ to our old life but to be raised with Christ to live out His resurrection life here and now. We need to continue in this ongoing battle *by faith,* as we believe the Word and minister that Word (4:13).
f) By keeping our eyes firmly on the unseen but eternal Christ, we will be equipped and sustained in the warfare against Satan and his demons (4:18).

Outcomes: As we live obediently to these challenges and promises in the midst of warfare, so we will be daily renewed (4:16) and able to realise that *all of this*, including the tough battles, are actually 'for your benefit, so that the grace that is reaching more and more people may cause thanksgiving to overflow to the glory of God' (4:15).

CH 5 ***Problem Manifested:*** The ministry of reconciliation granted to believers has a horizontal as well as vertical dimension. The horizontal nature of this ministry involves Christian engagement in seeking to diffuse tension, disagreement, division, all of which are rooted ultimately in the work of invisible dark powers operating in this world. The work of Satan and his demons is never far below the surface of the 2 Cor. text, even if they are not explicitly mentioned. In 5:5, we are told that God has given us the Spirit as a deposit, guaranteeing what is to come. In 5:9 the Apostle Paul makes the general statement that our goal as active believers in the Lord is 'to please Him, whether we are at home in the body or away from it'. In 5:10 we are informed that at the judgment seat of Christ we will be judged for the things done in the body, whether good or bad. These three truths are guaranteed by God's Word but at the same time they guarantee that we will face opposition from the Enemy whenever we attempt actively to obey these truths. The same sort of conflict will arise whenever we oppose the human pride that Satan seeks to foster (5:12-13), and whenever we try to live for Christ (5:15). Wherever Christians engage with a fallen world in the task of reconciliation, both vertical and horizontal, there *will* be simultaneous engagement with spiritual powers (5:16-21).

Enemy Strategy: We have already seen in 2 Cor 3:14 that Satan is capable of creating spiritual dullness of mind for those locked into Old Covenant thinking. Likewise, Paul tells us in 2 Cor 4:4 that the 'god of this age has blinded the minds of unbelievers' so that they cannot see and understand spiritual truth. For both situations, such blind people need the work of Christ and Spirit to release them from such bondage. It is also true that Satan and his workers seek to conceal, minimise or distort vital areas of biblical truth, even from the members of the Church itself!

Weapons/Resources: Thus for example, there seems little awareness in the wider Church of the goal of God in preparing believers to receive a covering with a resurrected body and with the future glory that God has prepared for us (2 Cor 5:1-5). The Corinthians were hugely ignorant in this area of the resurrection body and so are we today! Satan conceals the truth that at the close of the age, Christians will be re-clothed with either transformed or resurrected bodies fit for life in the new heavens and the new earth. Such confidence and assurance is certainly not Satan's desire for believers! Here and now we receive a foretaste of the Spirit but the fullness will be granted in the hereafter. The true Word of God cannot be broken and the Spirit of God who dwells within us can be trusted to lead us safely into the presence of God at the point of our passing away from this death.

Paul then writes in 5:12-13 about his absence of any need for letters of recommendation, since the Corinthians themselves were his endorsement (3:1-3). He is not interested in promoting his own cause in any way but would prefer the church members to tell his proud opponents how much they appreciated authentic gospel ministers. In short, Paul wants the Corinthians to take a solid stand against his enemies, the false teachers, who were boasting of their own achievements. The false apostles were having a negative and destructive influence on this church and Paul sees a place for God's people actively to oppose proud and arrogant enemies of the gospel by defending Paul and speaking against the devious and demonic claims of the intruders in Corinth. Paul wants the church not to keep their mouths shut but rather verbally to challenge the powerless, attainment-centred boasting of the false teachers and preachers in Corinth. In 2 Cor 5:12 the apostle Paul is attacking the mentality of the demonically-driven false apostles that the externals are all that matter. They were valuing their letters of commendation (3:1), Jewish heritage (11:22), visions and revelations (12:1), eloquence of speech (10:10; 11:6) and the performance of miracles (12:12). Satan loves the externals that do nothing to impress the God who looks on the heart instead. It is tempting for us to seek praise for ourselves but such praise of and for ourselves ultimately fails to glorify God and simply plays into the hands of our great enemy. Christ Himself delivered a huge challenge – "So you also, when you have done everything you were told to do, should say, 'We are unworthy servants; we have only done our duty'" (Luke 17:10). Paul follows this up in 5:13 by showing how even his spectacular divine vision of the third heaven (12:2) didn't actually do anything to help his ministry to people. For the latter he needed to be fully in control of his senses. Paul thus attacks the false claims of his opponents concerning their revelations! He was fully committed to resolute, sacrificial discipleship and dealt ruthlessly with any demonic distractions that might damage his Christian life and ministry.

Outcomes: We learn lessons of great importance in this Chapter 5. Paul is showing the Corinthian Church the diverse means by which Satan seeks to undermine and damage the community of believers. The apostle is very aware of Satan's arsenal of destructive tricks to cause discord, deception, division and disunity in the Church. His key method to diffuse and remove the potential discord and damage from the intruders is by frequently reminding his readers of the true nature of the gospel of Christ and this he does systematically and particularly in 5:14-6:2 – the ministry of reconciliation. In 5:14, Paul confesses that Christ controls him and all believers. This is in sharp contrast to his opponents in Corinth who are actually controlled by their own selfish ambitions. It was on the Cross of Calvary that the Christ delivered the deathblow to death, thus setting His people free from the bondage of sin – see Romans 6:6-7. We 'died' with Him at the Cross and are incorporated into the Body of Christ. Such theological reality is total anathema to the powers of darkness – a truth that those powers will fight and fight to deny and destroy, if only they could! The battle with these powers will be long and hard because of 5:15 – Christ's death for us and our 'death' with Him are intended to produce a lifelong relationship of intimate fellowship with Christ – see Romans 14:7-8. This is the reality that Satan hates with a vengeance and he will work constantly to undermine it by a range of subtle and not-so-subtle ways. Not surprising really, for through Christ's death and resurrection we have been delivered from sin, death and bondage to the dark dominion of Satan, in order that we will live in the resurrection kingdom of light in this life and beyond, dwelling and serving God in the eternal presence and glory of Christ.

Paul continues in 5:16 to show how the work of Christ universally changes His Church. Paul, on his conversion, changed his way of thinking about the Christ that he had probably seen in the streets of Jerusalem. No longer do Christians think in their pre-conversion worldly ways. Christ has torn us out of Satan's kingdom and ways of thinking and that divine transformation of believers' lives will be hugely resented and opposed continually by the evil powers of Satan. For example, new and indeed mature believers will struggle with temptation as they live the new life of a new creation in Christ and in Christian community. They will need to plead the 6th petition of the Lord's Prayer – 'And lead us not into temptation, but deliver us from the evil one,' (Matt 6:13) – and realise in their own experience that God will indeed supply the strength to resist evil. The wonder is that God took the initiative to restore the relationship between Himself and us in order that His work of new creation could be fully implemented. God did not cause the alienation and thus was under no obligation to reconcile Himself to us, and yet because of His love, God, the offended party, takes it upon Himself to reconcile us to Himself through the atoning work of His Son, the Lord Jesus Christ. All this is the work of the Holy Spirit by which God achieves new creation – reconciliation – restoration – righteousness – peace, and it is a work that will trigger ongoing opposition from the powers of darkness. Why? Because this cosmic ministry and message of reconciliation has been entrusted by God into the hands of weak, frail and dependent men and women (5:18-20).

The Church will be Satan's target for attack as he tries to stop this divine message of reconciliation doing its powerful and transformative work in the lives of individuals and communities. Indeed those called to be ambassadors for Christ (5:20) will be thrust into the arena of opposition from invisible but powerful demonic forces. Scripture makes it clear that human beings do play a part in their repentance and conversion. God does the calling but we must respond and answer and it is in the whole process of people coming to faith that Satan will seek to inject his maximum interference to mess up a good outcome!

The ultimate demonstration of the love of God was when God had His Son pay the death penalty for our sins (5:21). Kistemaker (1997:200) put it like this – 'an earthly judge does not bear any personal animosity toward a person who is accused, proven guilty, and sentenced. Nor does the judge establish a friendship with an offender. This is not so between God and the sinner… Through him (Christ), God imputed to his people righteousness, extended to them his friendship, and effected peace between himself and them.' Jesus was tempted by Satan but never slipped into sin. When God finally made Christ sin by imputing to him our sin, he regarded him as the sinbearer, not as a sinner. By imputing sin to Christ, God imputes righteousness to his people. God thus accepts us because our sin has been removed, and now treats us as if we had never sinned at all. We are declared innocent because of Christ's death. In Luke 4, Satan repeatedly challenged Christ concerning his Sonship for it was by the death of God's Son that sin, death and Satan were dealt a final blow and the powers and principalities were disarmed. No surprise therefore that Satan still seeks to undermine believing faith in the atoning death and bodily resurrection of the Christ!

The Enemy's attacks will not be occasional only, for 6:1 gives us a present tense of the infinitive to show that the hard work of receiving God's grace is continuous – the time for preaching and teaching is continuous and so therefore is the duration of demonic opposition also continuous for the people of God. Satan will continually find ways of preventing people from responding positively to the preached Word of God. Paul makes it very clear in 6:1-2 that the need for the Corinthians to repent and be reconciled to God is immediate and urgent. Time is short and the opportunity for the Corinthians to act is also limited. Satan's restricted authority, influence and freedom is also determined by God Almighty, but the reality is that Satan *does* have a degree of permitted power. The battle is truly on in heavenly places but is worked out here in *our*lives and situations!

<u>CH 6</u> ***Problem Manifested:*** In verses 3-10 Paul lists his struggles and persecutions, no doubt demonically inspired, and in verse 7 he specifically makes reference to 'weapons of righteousness in the right hand and in the left'. In verses 11-18 the apostle refers to 'wickedness', 'darkness', 'Belial', 'unbelievers', 'temple of idols', all of which relate in various ways to the demonic. In 7:1, the call to purify themselves from contamination again involves the demonic world.

Enemy Strategy: It comes as no surprise that following the glory of the New Covenant gospel and its reconciling power spelled out in 5:16-6:2, Paul immediately launches into a warning mode from 6:2-7:1. The apostle is no stranger to the tactics of the enemy through his efforts at discrediting the gospel and the Church, through many and various methods of attack. Paul is calling on all believers to be aware of the dangers but especially those in positions of leadership and Bible Training ministry. All who minister the gospel of Christ must make special efforts to be blameless in their lives and ministries so that our ministries are not discredited. Anyone who proclaims the Word of God but fails to practice its teachings will be wide open to the accusations of the world and the efforts of the devil to trip up ministers, evangelists and leaders in particular. We are warned to remove any reason that may provide an opportunity for people to find offence in the lives of serving Christians (6:3). Satan works overtime, given such opportunities, to produce maximum damage for gospel and Church! Down the centuries, Satan has scored many victories in this way, for when a minister of the Word breaks God's moral law enshrined in that Word, then the Church's witness to the world is at 'best' reduced in its effectiveness or at worst utterly paralyzed or totally destroyed. It is simply catastrophic in its consequences!

Weapons/Resources: Paul's strategy for avoiding such disasters is to affirm that he and his workers are servants of the Lord with delegated authority to serve in His name. He is thus able to commend himself with regard to his ministry – and a very costly ministry it was in so many ways for this apostle to the Gentiles. So much of 2 Cor 6:4ff is then a personal testimony from Paul to God's character and intervention in Paul's life, by which his ministry was used of the Lord and he himself was sustained and preserved in the midst of so many assaults from the varied enemies against his life and ministry. In 6:4-5 Paul faced a range of physical, mental and spiritual challenges and needed to exercise God-given perseverance to come through them. Following this group of nine hardships/afflictions, Paul then lists 8 gifts of God in 6:6-7a – purity, knowledge, patience, kindness, Holy Spirit, genuine love, word of truth, power of God. In 6:7b-8, the apostle Paul uses three clauses that deal with the concept of going 'through'. Just as a soldier stands between weapons on his right and left, so Paul and his co-workers stand between glory and dishonour, bad report and good report. We all have access in Christ and by the Spirit to the weapons of spiritual warfare – see Rom 13:12; 2 Cor 6:7; 10:4; Eph 6:13-18; 1 Thess 5:8. The kinds of weapons are not specified at this point but the right hand would have held the sword/spear for offensive warfare, whilst the left hand would have gripped the shield for defense. Verse 7b could refer to the weapons that righteousness supplies or the weapons that promote righteousness. It could mean uprightness of character, moral strength and holiness of life, but also could refer to a defensive tactic against Christ's critics, as well as offensive strikes to destroy enemy strongholds and to capture people's thought for Christ (10:4-5). Paul moves from one spiritual battle to another, sometimes receiving honour and good reports; sometimes slander! Yet in the midst of all of this, he takes his stand very firmly on the ministry of the Word of God. You win some and you lose some, as the saying goes! Many Corinthians appreciated his ministry (1 Cor 16:15-18) but others sought to discredit him and murmur behind his back (1 Cor 4:10-13, 19; 2 Cor 10:10; 11:7).

Finally in 6:8b-10, Paul introduces seven sets of contrasting hardships in which he presents himself as being 'knocked down', as it were, but then consist-ently and repeatedly getting back on his feet! For example, the slanderers accused Paul of being deceivers, as Jesus was similarly accused by the chief priests; yet Paul's character shone out. He faced a number of near-death experiences; yet his life was repeatedly spared. He was constantly sustained by the life of the risen Christ. It was the divine power that raised Christ from the dead that preserved Paul from dying a premature death. Our adversities are actually God's discipline and correction to bring us closer to the Lord Himself. God's constant loving care keeps Paul safe even though he suffered much pain in beatings. Somehow, in the strength of God, he stays cheerful and joyful even in the midst of sorrow.

In 6:11-13, Paul reaffirms his deep love for this congregation and his consistent willingness to preach and teach the gospel with complete openness, sincerity and authenticity. His use of words here suggests that although he and his workers have great love for the church in Corinth – 'you Corinthians', 'my children' – there is unfortunately a degree of narrow-mindedness, lack of love and threads of suspicion among the Corinthians. Paul wants the church to reciprocate his love for them! He wants them to accept him in love, in the same way he has accepted them!

In the following section, 6:14-7:1, the apostle Paul essentially makes the point that there should be no making of covenant relationships with unbelievers that water down or violate the covenant relationships that a believer has with God through Christ. Unbelievers at root have been blinded by Satan (2 Cor 4:4) and as such are not yet related to the Lord in any meaningful way. Believers must reject deception in all its forms because it is rooted in the rule of Satan and must be rejected at all costs. Light and righteousness are intimately connected; both are at polar extremes from darkness and lawlessness. Paul notes elsewhere that Satan can and does transform himself into an angel of light (2 Cor 11:4) with the purpose of deceiving people! His work is to blind the minds of unbelievers in such a way that they cannot see the light of the gospel. Their lives are lived in a state of spiritual darkness, but God, in His grace and mercy, can and does shine his light into lives, bringing by Christ and Spirit the saving knowledge of Himself (2 Cor 4:4-6). In 6:15 we meet *Belial* who in Jewish writings is personified as 'Satan', 'the devil', 'the highest demon' and 'the antichrist'. Paul in his 2nd Corinthian letter so far had placed heavy emphasis on the death of Christ, God's work of reconciling the world to Himself and Paul's own sufferings in the cause of this gospel of Christ. Now he challenges his readers in Corinth to choose and follow this Christ, whilst at the same time turning their backs and rejecting *Belial* in all his ugly forms and ways. Paul is *not* saying that believers must have no contact at all with unbelievers but rather that they must not share in their attitudes, actions and lifestyles. God, writes Paul, has already revealed His power against the idols of pagan gods and now demands that Christian believers must withdraw from participation in the sacrifices of pagan temples and shrines. Such sacrifices were offered to demons and not to God (1 Cor 10:20). The OT texts referred to here carry the idea of the need for God's people to live pure lives. Embedded in this text is the remarkable truth that the triune God – Father Son and Holy Spirit – dwells in the hearts of believers! Great assurance here for our engagement in the heat and intensity of spiritual warfare (2 Cor 6:16b). The following verse 17 makes clear God's demand that the covenant people of His possession absolutely must keep their promises to God and be obedient to His Word. Our commitment to Christ has to be unwavering and as long as we uphold that demand, then the Lord God Almighty will sustain us in our Satanic warfare. Our deep personal relationship with the Godhead that rules over this cosmos is further mentioned in 6:18. We call Him 'Father' – for that is who and what He is – but that means we must never fall into the defilement of idolatry. This demands the utmost holiness and dedication from us if we are to fight in God's battles.

Outcomes: The lesson is surely that even through intense spiritual warfare, Paul is actually enriched, preserved and strengthened in faith. The attempts of Satan to bring him down consistently fail and it is the Lord God, not Satan and his demon armies, who fulfills His kingdom purposes, even in the direst of Paul's highly stressful circumstances. That great truth emerges as a key outcome from 6:1-10, but then it is also clear from verses 14-18 that God is indeed 'Almighty' and the omnipotent One beyond all comparison, whether in heaven or on earth. No one and no thing can ever touch Him or come anywhere near Him. We however are vulnerable, and especially so in the context of spiritual warfare! Yet here is how 7:1 comes to our aid since we are the beloved children of the living God, and that Almighty God is totally committed to fulfilling His promises. Yet because of our proneness to sin, we must ask forgiveness and cleansing on a continual basis. Those believers who engaged in sacrificial cult were very likely to come under the temptation of involvement with cult prostitutes. As active believers we must continually seek sanctification and its goal of complete holiness, based on and rooted in our fear and reverence for God. The lord's holiness should be reflected in our own lives. This will then function as our massive weapon from the Lord in our spiritual battles with all forms of temptation in this fallen world. Let us never forget that we as Christians are God's temple, because the Lord Himself is living in us and walking among us!

CH 7 Paul describes his ministry in Macedonia in verse 5 as 'this body of ours had no rest, but we were harassed at every turn – conflicts on the outside, fears within'. Further evidence of Satan's continual disruptive activity as he tries to plunge God's workers into a state of feeling 'downcast' (v. 6) – that negative emotional territory always favoured for occupation by enemy forces. Verse 13 mentions 'encouragement' cf 'downcast' in verse 6. The battle involves our emotions.

<u>**CH 8**</u> In verse 20-21 Paul explains the safeguards he wants to set in place re the Jerusalem Collection to ensure that no criticism is provoked over this whole venture. He wants to avoid allowing any opportunity for Satan to interfere and mess up the collection plan that will ultimately demonstrate the unity and love of a Church that is both Jew and Gentile. That will be the chief witness/testimony of such a Collection, but Paul appoints trustworthy men to accompany the collection to make the plan successful by God's enabling.

<u>**CH 9**</u> Again Paul repeats in verses 1-5 that he is sending two brothers to ensure the collection procedure moves along well, without any interference from possible disruption. Great glory is going to God through this collection and Paul doesn't want anything, or any demonic powers, to stop the successful completion of the Jerusalem Collection.

<u>**CH 10**</u> Christians are not to live their lives by the standards of this world (10:2). In verse 3 Paul writes that there is a war going on, but in verse 4 he stresses that our weapons of warfare are *not* those of this world but rather weapons that have 'divine power to demolish strongholds'. In particular in verses 5-6, the apostle has the goal to 'demolish arguments and every pretension that sets itself up against the knowledge of God, and we take captive every thought to make it obedient to Christ. And we will be ready to punish every act of disobedience, once your obedience is complete.'

<u>**CH 11**</u> Even as early in the chapter as verse 3, Paul is referring to the deception of Eve by the serpent and the way in which some Corinthian minds had been led astray by that deception away from devotion to Christ. Verse 4 confirms the presence of a different Jesus, Spirit and gospel by such deception from the enemy forces. Paul becomes even more specific and personal in 11:13-15 by exposing these human agents as deceivers who are in fact 'false apostles, deceitful workmen, masquerading as apostles of Christ'. Indeed, says the apostle, Satan himself appears as an angel of light. Such men will be finally condemned in their pretense to be servants of righteousness. The references to 'enslavement', 'exploitation', 'taking advantage', 'pushing forward', 'slapping in the face', 'boasting' all hint at evil powers. The section on Paul's sufferings in 11:23-29 also is set against the 'invisible' background of evil powers at work.

CH 12 Because of the great revelations made to Paul, he received a thorn in his flesh – a messenger of Satan – to torment him. Ultimately this thorn came by God's own permission in order to keep Paul in weakness and thereby demonstrate divine power in Paul's weakness (12:7-10). Paul's ongoing fears for this church are that he will find more evidence of evil powers at work in and through some Corinthians, namely 'quarrelling', 'jealousy', 'anger', 'factions', 'slander', 'gossip', arrogance', 'disorder', 'impurity', 'sexual sin', 'debauchery' (12:20-21).

CH 13 A world of evil influences lies behind Paul's reminder that two or three witnesses are required,since the absence of such witnesses could open the way to unfairness, prejudice and demonically-inspired judgments and decisions over church matters (13:1). Likewise in verse 8, the maintenance of *Truth* at all times reminds the readers that Satan is profoundly opposed to divine truth.

REFLECTION ON SATANIC STRATEGIES IN 2nd Corinthians

Based on the text and contexts of 2 Corinthians and through Paul's perspective, teaching and personal experiences, it seems that the dark world of supernatural powers operates in a number of different ways –

God operates at both ends of the spectrum of suffering and comfort, as well as along the spectrum itself. Warfare involves the divine, the demonic and the human, but because those worlds are in a real sense invisible, it becomes very hard to disentangle the relative roles of the 'contributors'. The powers of darkness will constantly seek to undermine the lives and ministries of Christians and churches and sometimes we make our own human contribution to that whenever we surrender to the pulls of the world, the flesh and the devil. God however remarkably is able to work in and through that matrix to bring glory to Himself. See Job 1-2; 2 Cor 12:7-10. Demonic powers are limited by God in their exercise of freedom to act. Our starting point and finishing point is always the absolute authority, power, control and compassion that God exercises in Christ's ultimate victory and by the work of His Spirit.

It is clear at a number of places in 2 Cor and elsewhere that Satan operates particularly effectively in messing up personal relationships, and especially so among Christian believers. He loves to exploit weaknesses in our personalities and flaws in our self-orientated attitudes and actions. Wherever there are divisions and discord between people, Satan will try to deepen and widen those rifts for as long as he possibly can until the maximum damage has been done. He is ultimately behind all discord and disunity in the Church. He also likes to go to extremes eg over the issue of believers who either try to exercise excessive discipline or who fail to discipline at all! Satan will force people to focus everything on grace or every thing on works, instead of believers holding *both together* in belief and practice!

Scripture affirms that Satan, the prince of this world, works constantly to hold men and women in spiritual darkness out of fear that they will gain and experience life-changing knowledge of God. Effective biblical teaching, preaching and training will always be opposed very strongly by dark forces, and this goes right back to the place of truth and deception in the early chapters of Genesis.

Satan works in our minds but also in our emotions to trigger discouragement, depression, darkness and despondency. Human, physical causes of course need to be considered alongside demonic intervention. Physical, mental, emotional and spiritual weakness so often work together, as Satan watches for opportunities to bring us as low as he can.

Satan and his forces have a degree of power to control and coordinate circumstances, opposition, persecution, so as to inflict the most damage to believers and churches. He will pile troubles onto us until we are in bondage to our fears for our survival in difficulties and feelings that we are drowning in our struggle to maintain trust in the love and power of the Living God amidst desperate circumstances. Satan concentrates his efforts within us – in our minds, bodies and emotions – but at the same time he will use other people, especially Christians, as well as our surrounding circumstances, to employ a 'triple whammy' of techniques, causing the sort of despair that will make us feel like giving up on Christian life and ministry. At the same time, our enemy will inject negative and evil thoughts into our minds regarding the trustworthiness of the Godhead amidst all our struggles.

Paul is very careful to set safeguards to protect the organisation and transportation of the Jerusalem Collection. He forward-plans the possible points at which enemy forces might intervene and disrupt the successful completion of the collection eg. possible apathy from the Corinthians, disagreement over methods, temptation to steal from the collection, danger from robbers en route, risk of pride from the Corinthians and/or lack of humility to accept the proffered help by those in Jerusalem. Many are the chances that Satan would seek to take to spoil the whole thing.

The apostle focuses in chapter 10 on the weapons we have to engage the enemy – the Word of God, the Spirit of God, our intercession with God. He is very aware that Satan will do all in his limited power to stifle *Knowledge of God* for that is the knowledge that will bring unbelievers to saving faith and transform their ongoing lives and ministries. God *has* provided weapons for our use in warfare. We aim in divine strength to capture minds that will then change minds and emotions, opening the way for believers to set their wills and actions in the new direction of obedience to God. This will *always* be opposed because Satan is fundamentally opposed to divine truth.

Satan was always a *Deceiver* and he sets the pattern for men and women who live in bondage to him. They may not always be aware of it but false apostles are actually mimicking their leaders in their own ministries of *Deception* that have produced a 'different Jesus, Spirit and Gospel'. This is a great warning about the subtlety of deception. The methods of reaching heaven put forward by the false teachers in Colossae (Col 2:6-23) sounded authentically Christian but were actually a deception that could never deliver the goods of a transformed life.

Satan exploits the fallen nature of humanity, and however much our sinful nature might have been redeemed by the Spirit's work, the old nature is still active and ready to rear its ugly head, producing the sort of Sins *within the Church* that Paul lists his fears about in 2 Cor 12:20-21.

Satan did have the permitted power to send a 'messenger' to Paul in the form of a thorn that troubled the apostle physically, mentally and emotionally for a very long time, even though it was from God that Paul sought delivery – 2 Cor 12:7-10. Satan can and does interfere at every level of our lives, but the Lord God Almighty has the ultimate power, victory and control to work all things to His praise and glory.

<u>Sermon 6</u> is a 'link' from sermons 1-5 into sermons 7-10, to try to establish just what is meant by 'overcoming' in Rev 2-3 and 12:10 and how that might connect with spiritual warfare.

<u>Sermons 7-10</u> show how we might engage in that warfare to prove that we are indeed 'overcomers' and hence the recipients of God's salvation in Christ.

SPIRITUAL WEAPONS:

6 Our Challenge to be 'Overcomers'

We seek now to investigate the nature of *overcoming* for believers and checking out the possible link(s) between *overcoming* and *spiritual warfare*. Who is overcoming, what or whom is being overcome – and how?
Let's begin our enquiry with the Trinity that we are most familiar with – the Father, The Son (Lord Jesus Christ) and the Holy Spirit.

The Scriptures reveal another 'Trinity' which actually tries to counterfeit that Holy Trinity, namely the Evil Trinity of Satan (the dragon or devil), the Anti-Christ (the beast) and the False Prophet (the beast coming out of the earth in Revelation 13). These two Trinities need to be explored in order to discover what on earth they have got to do with the issue that most concerns us, namely Spiritual Warfare. Let's start with the world we are most familiar with today.

What is the meaning of 'the world' in which we now live?
Let's begin to answer this question of *overcoming* by starting here and now in the world in which we live and move and have our being. We believe we know and understand and experience this present world that we now inhabit, but let's go back initially to a cluster of biblical verses that reveal another Trinity – The *world*, the *flesh* and the *devil*. These are mentioned to varying degrees in Joshua 9; Romans 7; James 3:15; 4:7-10 and 1 John 2:16. Satan basically and primarily operates secretly, covertly and deceitfully through the world and the flesh. The word 'world' in its biblical usage actually refers to society that has deleted, ignored or eliminated God in any meaningful sense. The challenges and temptations faced by Christians come from this godless 'world' through the influence of media, peer group, work mates, office culture, friends or gangs.

1 John 2:15f declares "Do not love the world or the things in the world. If any one loves the world, love for the Father is not in him". John continues to list what he sees in this godless world – 'the lust of the flesh, the lust of the eyes, and the pride of life, is not of the Father but is of the world". He sees the world as "lying in the power of the wicked one" (1 John 5:19). The children of this world and the children of God are radically different, the one group from the other. The world does not know Christians because the world does not know God (1 John 3:1). The Spirit of God within us is a force more powerful than the world and can enable us to resist the

downward pull of the world (1 John 4:4, 5:4). Satan tries his best to persuade us to "walk according to the course of this world" (Eph 2:2). That should not surprise us in the slightest because Satan is "the god of this world" (2 Cor 4:4).

What is the meaning of 'the flesh'?

The term 'flesh' could be as easily misunderstood as the term 'world', because the normal usage of 'flesh' in the New Testament does not refer to the human, physical body. Rather is it a term that is used to refer to the weakness, frailty and sinfulness of humanity, especially as used in Paul's letters. There is a continual battle between the Spirit and the flesh of a believer. The war is ongoing (Galatians 5:17; Ephesians 2:3). The flesh is very prone to cave in to evil suggestions and to be influenced by the tempting attractions of the world. The Apostle Paul nearly despaired in Romans 7:18 when he wrote, "I know that nothing good lives in me, that is in my flesh". He sought to serve the law of God in his mind, but he was frequently pulled into serving the law of sin with his flesh (Rom 7:25)!

All believers experience this 'dualism' within themselves… and struggle! Indeed we are called to *crucify* the flesh with its passions and desires (Gal 5:24). Yes, we have forgiveness and freedom in Christ, but not the freedom to indulge the flesh in sinful thoughts, feelings and actions (Gal 5:13.) We are called by God to change our clothing and to put on the Lord Jesus Christ and give no allowance whatsoever to the flesh (Rom 13:4).

In short *the flesh within us is as fickle and as dangerous as the world around us.* All three – the world, the flesh and the devil – will work together to drag us down into the depths of sin, if we allow or encourage such an evil cocktail of influences to influence and impact us.

What is the meaning of 'the devil' and the 'demonic'?

When human beings use the term 'demonic', it is generally intended to refer to shocking human events, such as mass shootings in schools that cause catastrophic numbers of deaths and injuries. We call it 'absolutely demonic' and we feel horrified by such events. The Scriptures would endorse our sense of outrage. However, we need to delve deeper into the actual Scriptural teaching on the 'demonic'.

The Bible clearly teaches that God Himself and God Alone is the root and source of *all things.* He created the universe and human beings, but also heavenly beings *ie.* the angels or messengers of God. The divine plan is that redeemed and resurrected Christian believers share a heavenly existence with the holy angels of God. The latter consists of the archangel Michael

(Jude 9), seraphim and cherubim (Gen 3:24; Isa 6:2ff), principalities, powers, thrones, authorities (Eph 1:21; 3:10; Col 1:16; 2:10; 1 Peter 3:22). These beings encircle the throne of God in worship. They also offer to give warnings, promises and protection (Matt 1:20; Luke 1:26; Gen 18:1-5; 19:1ff). Scripture reveals the presence of angels at Jesus' birth, His resurrection and at His return in judgment (Mk 8:38; Matt 25:31; 2 Thess 1:7). Angels feature at a number of places through Scripture: the giving of the Law (Acts 7:53; Gal 3:19); in Jesus's teaching (Lk 16:22; Matt 13:39); in the mission role of the church, accompanied by its suffering and persecution (1 Cor 4:9; Rom 8:38; Eph 3:9f; 1 Peter 1:12; Heb 12:22; 1 Tim 3:16).

However, *it is also the case that Satan owns disciples from the angelic realms.* Such evil beings have been thrown by God into darkness and will come under divine judgment (2 Peter 2:4; Jude 6). When Satan rebelled against God, followers from among the heavenly beings must somehow have declared their allegiance to the Devil and joined him in his rebellion and fall. They worked under the lead of Satan in his kingdom of darkness to do all they could to delay, damage or, if it were possible, destroy God's Kingdom of Light. These demonic forces seek to persuade human beings also to join the Enemy ranks and wreak disruption and damage across the globe. Struggling, confused and backsliding Christian believers are at risk of contributing to, or even joining in, those who work more directly in the ranks of demonic powers. All too often, confessing Christians submit themselves to the influence and suggestions of demonic powers and thereby cause great damage to the cause of the Gospel and Church! We need constantly to remind ourselves of the Reformed evangelical preacher and minister Dr Martin Lloyd Jones who wrote the following – "The first thing we have to realise is that the Christian life is a warfare, that we are strangers in an alien land, that we are in the enemy's territory.... The teaching which gives the impression that the pathway to glory is all easy and simple and smooth is not Christianity".

So where does this investigation into the "world, the flesh and the devil" leave us with regard to its relevance to our engagement in Spiritual Warfare? Believers are under constant attack from these three directions. Paul in his letters, especially Ephesians and Colossians, gives us huge detail and direction about our need to deal with these assaults from Satan. We are indeed called to resist Satan, equip our new selves and overcome all Satan's efforts to 'reclaim' us!

What is the meaning of 'Overcome' in Revelation 2-3?
Before we look at this material in our sermon preparation, and eventually in our delivery of this message to our listeners, we surely need to take very serious account of Revelation Chapter One. Rev 1 is literally packed with biblical truth that prepares readers and listeners to engage confidently in Spiritual Warfare, whether in the first century AD, or here and now in the 21st! Let's view some examples drawn briefly from the text of Rev 1:

Rev 1:1-3 – Here we are assured that the Lord Jesus Christ is the central figure in the Revelation to John. The message comes from the Father to Jesus to an angel to John to the churches. It comes from the Godhead and it absolutely focuses on Christ or the message or both. The 'John' is most probably the apostle, the son of Zebedee and this man had personally known Jesus in the flesh cf. John 21:22. John testifies to what he has seen, namely the word of God and the testimony of Jesus Christ (Rev 1:2). Very significantly, John identifies with us as a 'servant' who 'suffers' in his own experience of discipleship. He shares with us in the areas of his absolute dependence on the Holy Spirit, his humility as a fellow-disciple and his obedience as a proclaimer of the gospel in a hostile world. This 'trinity' of identity with us is precisely what gave him, and still gives, a whole 'shedful' of trouble. Why? Because it thrusts us into the heated centre of Spiritual Warfare! These believers in the seven churches were caught up by two major challenges – persecution by the State and temptation to compromise with this world. Satan and his armies were involved at both of these levels of their lives. Nevertheless, God is completely in control and is working out his good and great purposes, rooted in His overwhelming love for us. God is absolutely a God of justice, but we must act in a just manner. We must beware of our own complacency and compromise in life. We must bow to the huge authority of God that is revealed in Revelation. We must not fall in love with the possessions and allegiances that this world offers us, but rather be constantly taking opportunities to proclaim this glorious saving gospel of Christ – this will give us pains.

Rev 1:4-8 – This section clearly shows how God is far greater and far more powerful than the tests that come into our lives during warfare. God is warning the churches that their suffering will not go away, but that the Godhead would by suffering equip us for a greater holiness. This passage strongly affirms the deity of Christ. We have the Trinity on our side in the battles we attract to us by godly life and ministry. It is because of our allegiance to Christ that we become embroiled in Spiritual Warfare but the Godhead sees that and comes to our aid! Christ Himself is the "faithful and true witness" and precisely because of that, we can utterly depend on His promises in the midst of battles. See Rev 3:14. Christ is our model for dealing with Spiritual Warfare. Even a martyr's death should not fill us with terror, because Jesus *was* the 'firstborn from the dead'. Not only will He raise us from death, but He loves us, frees us from sin and makes us a kingdom and priests.

The text of Revelation also assures the suffering saints that He will personally return to exercise His perfect justice, especially on those who have persecuted Christ's Church. Emperor Caesar had only limited power over Christians; Christ alone ruled supremely in time, space and cosmos and the lives – and deaths – are firmly in His hands. Christ is the One 'who was, who is and who is to come'. Again, this is the assurance we need in our own troubles and testings, when we may lose our sense of God's presence and parenthood. This is the time to reflect on His deep, deep love in dying and then rising for us. This love *continues.* It's not just past but is present and future. He alone is truly in control of our lives, even when we feel we are losing in the Spiritual Warfare. God is never taken by surprise in the events of our lives. Nothing ever catches Him off His guard.

Rev 1:9-12 – John further reveals and reinforces our need for fortitude and endurance as we go through the suffering that will bring us the kingdom. After all, John had been exiled to the Island of Patmos as a punishment imposed by the Roman State. Why? Because he had refused *to cease preaching and testifying about Jesus.* See Rev 6:9; 12:11. Banishment meant profound humiliation, loss of freedom and indeed, the loss of a victim's sense of honour. Much of the exile was spent in deep suffering and hardship, until death intervened. John's exile was probably less severe than this, but far from easy as an older man. Exile was very common in Domitian's reign, often because Christians worshipped the True *kurios* – Lord – and refused to bow the knee to 'Lord Caesar'! John seems to have been in worship 'in the Spirit' when the vision came. This likely happened when he was in worship that led to a visionary state. In the midst of pain, suffering and immense uncertainty, the Spirit of God intervened! John may well have written this vision down, even as he received it. The exciting reality was that Jesus *appeared among the lampstands* (churches). For John, each Christian congregation was a lampstand and for John, that probably pointed to the universal, global Church. John was very aware that Jesus stood – and still stands – solidly around all believers who suffer pain, loss and deep anguish, for their faith. The Spirit of God even equips us to worship God in the midst of the distress and agony of persecution and 'exile'. Prayer is integral.

One issue of great importance is that ministers need to be very sensitive and careful when they teach and preach about persecution, pain and all manner of problems, especially if their own experience is relatively mild in comparison with the deep challenges of others. Yes, God is with us in the persecution that will accompany our gospel and word proclamation, and we *will finally reign with Him* (Rom 8:17; 2 Tim 2:12). John is certainly up to his eyes in his sharing in the patient endurance of the tribulation that is indeed the way into the kingdom of God. Such suffering and martyrdom actually speeds up the end. Our commitment to Word, Prayer and Spirit will equip us for our greater effectiveness in Spiritual Warfare. It is to *all his people* worldwide that Jesus grants the massive privilege of being immersed in Spiritual Warfare, regardless of the consequences and sufferings.

Rev 1:13-20 – Here we surely reach what must be considered the climax of our preparation for Spiritual Warfare. John's vision presents Jesus, not only as King of the universe, but also as our own High Priest. The Christ is portrayed here as truly Christ in His glorified state, fully divine and fully risen. In short, He is all-powerful and as such able to empower and protect His own people in the face of their persecutors. God really is greater than our greatest trials. These are images from Daniel concerning the absolute glory of God. John wastes no time in describing this revelation of Christ Himself and especially draws our attention to Christ as Word. The Lord Jesus Christ is about to speak, but at this precise moment, John is stretched out on the ground (Rev 1:17). He is totally overwhelmed, but then come four words from Christ that are even more overwhelming, if that were possible! *"Do not be afraid"*. The vision to the seven churches and to all churches is about to be given to and through John… and he is told not to be afraid! Why oh why, on earth, should this God be so concerned about you and your church and what's happening in your church? OK, it's not actually your church, or my church or anybody's church. It's God's Church and Christ died and rose for His Church. That's how much He cares. That's how much He doesn't want you or me to be afraid of spiritual warfare! God underlines in this vision the deity of Christ. By His rising from the dead, Jesus absolutely guaranteed eternal life to all His disciples.

That's why we need not fear spiritual warfare. Christ holds the keys to death and life – the very two realms that fill people today with dreaded fear. Suicide is now in the UK the highest cause of death among the under-35 year olds! Death comes to us *only in the timing and the will of our Almighty Father.* That brings great comfort for those facing possible martyrdom under the Roman Empire and today. God cares deeply for His people and for every detail of their lives and deaths. Remarkably, the 'stars' in Rev 1:20 are most likely the guardian angels of individuals, congregations and leaders of congregations. The vision piles on, and on, the reasons not to fear.

God is able to handle our suffering by persecution, our economic testings, our temptations to compromise our faith, our fears over death and unexpected sickness and our anxiety over unemployment, loss, bereavement or unwarranted criticism from people. The future belongs to God, and His Church will finally prevail, even in, and through, the most dire of circumstances that might be imagined. The Godhead ultimately wins out, whatever the intensity of the spiritual warfare that the Church will encounter, even in the most dark days.

The specific significance of 'overcoming' in Rev 2-3

Each of the seven letters is a prophetic word from Jesus, but each church received the whole vision of the Book of Revelation. This word came through the Spirit who is inspiring John. The letters contained positives, negatives and a strong plea for churches, both then and now, to be open and attentive to what the Spirit is saying. In particular each church is warned of the crucial need to 'overcome'. It is to that word that we must now turn for understanding and obedience to its purpose, meaning and application both then and now.

2:1-7 Ephesus

The people of Ephesus would have been extremely aware of the dominance of the Roman Imperial Cult which demanded much from the population in terms of required allegiance to this evil cult. Ephesus was a centre of several major pagan religions, especially Emperor Cult and Diana – Artemis – Cult. It was also a focal point for the false teaching that was influencing the churches in the first century AD. It was a hotbed for Satanic presence and practice, and the church addressed by the Spirit was seriously lacking in love for God and people. The Spirit calls the church in Ephesus to repent and return. The Nicolaitans tolerated immorality and sacrificial eating. The Ephesian are told by the Spirit of God that if they want to 'overcome' *ie.* eat of the tree of eternal life, then they would not only have to maintain doctrinal orthodoxy, but also to display internal church unity through love. What a challenge to *all churches* today! Few churches seem to get that key balance in a healthy condition. How embarrassing for some churches to have their mail 'opened' and read by the other six churches, as well as each church receiving the entire Book of Revelation! The very idea of 'conquering' suggests the involvement of every believer and church in spiritual warfare, and the willingness of all believers to persevere in the forthcoming trials portrayed in the text of the rest of the Book of Revelation. The Ephesian Church, like all churches, needed to demonstrate transformed life to those immersed in the surrounding pagan culture. It is alarming when churches slowly take on board, adopt and live out the growing popularity of relative truth/ morality and material comfort! Some churches are tightly committed to the gospel and yet are at the same time, too dogmatic about issues that are secondary. We must surely never forget that churches – lampstands – can be removed, if they fail to love, to welcome, to teach, to persevere.

2:8-11 Smyrna

This city was heavily involved in Imperial Cult too. The Roman authorities for a while considered Christians as in some ways part of Judaism, and thus excused certain obligations to offer worship to Imperial Cult. However, some synagogue leaders began to build rifts with Christians, making persecution more likely for them. Smyrna was ruled by Asian Greeks, so the Jews had to work hard to keep good relations with the Greek population. 'Satan' is mentioned in this portion of the letter and some people claimed to be Jews but were actually working alongside local officials to betray, name and persecute Christians and make life as difficult as possible for them. Christians thus had to be faithful and ready for imprisonment, torture and possible death. Thus, in this context, Christians could be called to martyrdom, by which they would avoid the horrors of the 'second death' (Rev 2:11). The 'overcoming' in this church required withstanding persecution; surrender of our lives, rather than engaging in retaliatory hostility.

John's audience regarded their congregations as Jewish. The first Christians were Jewish and their earliest Gentile converts felt they were being converted to Judaism. Christians who venerated Scriptures and practiced fidelity were viewed as Jews. However, they viewed Jews who rejected Jesus as apostate from Israel's true faith. Jewish Christians thus felt that Jews had actually cut themselves off from their heritage in God's true covenant. Our heritage in biblical Judaism should be honoured, whilst we pray for the Spirit's enlightenment for the transformation of all people. 'Overcoming' requires serious counting up of the cost of true discipleship today. Only Smyrna and Philadelphia received clear commendation, mainly because of the suffering that fostered reflection, pain, dependence and purity. True overcoming is only possible by the strength that God Himself gives us. As ministers of the Gospel, the preparation of our people for possible martyrdom must include training to remain faithful disciples of Christ in the face of hatred, rejection and persecution. These are integral to our own spiritual warfare today.

2:12-17 Pergamum

These verses include two references to 'Satan'. The 'sword' may indicate the Roman authority to carry out capital punishment, in which case it may well be the case that Jesus is underlining that He alone holds and controls the power of life and death (1:18). This would encourage those undergoing persecution. Jesus certainly is stressing, though, that He is engaged in the warfare against false teachers who were damaging his church (2:15-16). Serpents were very familiar in Pergamum, where the healing cult of Asclepius was dominant and the altar of Zeus contained serpent sculptures. Both realities would have regularly reminded Pergamum inhabitants of the reality of Satan and the constant threat he posed to the church. This explains why Satan had his 'throne' in this city. To 'crown it all', Pergamum was a centre for Imperial Cult. Faithful witness Antipas was martyred here (2:13) and Jesus commends the faith/faithfulness of such martyrs.

Balaam in his greed led people astray into sinful activities like physical and spiritual adultery. Food offered to idols led believers into syncretism as they took part in other religions' practices, thus exposing themselves to compromise. Similarly, trade guilds insisted on members, including Christians, making sacrifices to other gods. Christians in this spiritual warfare needed to be ready for suffering and persecution. An obvious, but vital point here is that false teaching and ungodly living need to be opposed by *sound biblical teaching*. Yes, a significant part of our engagement in spiritual warfare needs to be carried out from our pulpits, our homes, our devotions and our study.

What form did 'overcoming' take in Pergamum? According to *Craig Keener* (2000:125) it meant "to continue steadfast in the face of opposition (2:13), but especially to stand against teachings of compromise with the world, and to do their best to purge such teachings from their ranks (2:14-16)." To the overcomers, Jesus promises 'hidden manna', probably referring to the Jewish tradition that the manna placed in the ark would be restored in the end time *ie.* eternal sustenance that required no labour. Also the gift of the white stone with a new name on it, probably a sort of entry 'pass' or 'ticket' to the messianic banquet in heaven. It could also well signify the hidden name of God and Lamb that true believers will carry forever.

The Church conquers by refusing to assimilate into godless world cultures, even in covert, subtle and insidious ways. How incredibly relevant is this in 2023! Yet, this is not the same as total withdrawal from culture! We need to influence this world with divine values, but to avoid adopting the world's values when they collide with the Kingdom's values. In the West we think we don't worship idols, yet we sometimes have an unhealthy and cosy relationship with secular materialism, celebrity cult and entertainment. We need to repent (2:16, 21-22). Whenever Christian leaders knowingly ignore, excuse or hide sin within the church, then they open the door to spiritual warfare that is actually self-inflicted.

The gospel *always* brings suffering (Mk 13:9-10; 2 Tim 3:12) and we must be ready for that, knowing that faithful witness to this world is essential before the Lord will return. We must have the Spirit's insight into those elements of our church life that involve compromise and be ready, with God's help, to avoid them like the plague. These include sexual immorality, subtle secularism, greed, obesity, dishonesty, personal relationships and a host of other issues. If as Christians we adopt the world's values and live by them, then we lose our distinctiveness and our witness in evangelism disappears. Never forget that Satan is a very capable theologian. He can twist the word 'love' into a multitude of meanings that justify *any relationship!* In the words of Keener (2000:131) "Revelation called the churches in Asia to wake up to the reality that the world and the church were locked in a fight to the death.... Whatever we must overcome, God has a better hope in store for us".

2:18-29 Thyatira

The main stress point in the Thyatira church seems to have involved economic issues that were pushing the church toward compromise over the need for believers to join trade guilds that required sacrifices to a range of deities and cults. 'Jezebel' falsely claimed to be a prophetess (2:20) who could offer 'deep secrets' (2:24). Under Satan, she deceived and misled God's servants into immorality of various sorts, including compromise with paganism. Divine judgment on Jezebel is promised in 2:22, and sickness plus personal tragedy crash in on Jezebel. This presence of false teaching in the Thyatira church is Jesus's only criticism of this church (2:23-24). The Spirit insists that the believers must hold fast to faith until Jesus returns. Jesus knows their very heart and mind and He is very aware that many in Thyatira have received their influences from Satan, who has also stirred up opposition from the synagogue folk in order to disturb this church. Jesus assures overcomers here of a share in His authority and reign over the nations, if they will resist false teaching. Yet again, our overcoming in spiritual warfare clearly includes our understanding, absorption and proclamation of the Divine Word. To this end, the Spirit will 'give' the Father and will give the 'morning star', namely Jesus Himself. The Trinity is our guarantee of success in the task of spiritual warfare today. Jesus is greater than the stars, who are angels of the churches.

In all of this issue of teaching, of course, we must make a distinction between what are matters of spiritual life and death, and what are the issues open to differences of opinion. Faithfulness to the Word of God is of absolutely fundamental importance and God *will* reward it. Far more important than wealth and status in this life is Jesus' approval of, and pleasure with, our lives on that Day of Judgment. One of the greatest dangers faced in Thyatira was the serious temptation for Christians to exercise a 'soft' love that tolerates all things and judges none whatsoever. Relativism and universalism are highly popular in postmodernity, whose definition for what is considered valid is best expressed by that term… '*whatever'!* As Keener wrote (2000:140) "…what kind of heavenly Father would send his own Son to the cross if the plan of salvation was actually multiple choice?" Orthodox Christian belief insists that remaining faithful until the very end (2:26) is an absolute requirement for eternal salvation. Many texts back this up –Acts 14:22; 1 Cor 9:27; 2 Cor 13:5; Col 1:23; 1 Thess 3:5; 1 Tim 4:1; Heb 2:1-4, 4:1-2, 6:4-8, 10:19-31, 12:14-17; James 5:19 - 20. Commitment to global mission is a complete non-negotiable, but it guarantees spiritual warfare for us.

3:1-6 Sardis

The sleeping church in Sardis is challenged to wake up. Pagan worship was rife here, especially in the worship of Demeter and the deified empress Livia. The Christians seem to have been sheltered from the real impact of persecution because they were sheltering under the wing of Jews who were protected by Rome. That makes it likely that they had settled comfortably into the ways of this world, thus making them feel spiritually drowsy and not clinging in dependence on God or pleading for His resurrection power. Only twice in its history had Sardis been conquered and only because the city had failed to be prepared. Hence Jesus warns Sardis to be prepared for

Him to come to them to shake them up. If the Sardians were ready to overcome the paganism of their culture, then they would walk in white with Jesus in the glories of the new Jerusalem! The reverse of this will be that many Sardians will slide into spiritual death and will fail to see the kingdom of God. A faithful remnant will nevertheless be saved for eternity (Mt 10:32; Lk 12:8).

We must beware of sliding into pagan culture that was underpinned by Satan. Instead we must all be awake and watchful, awaiting the Lord's return and judgment, concerning our overcoming of all the demonic efforts to damage, deflect and destroy the church of Christ. A key point here in the biblical text is the severe warning in 3:5 that those who fail to overcome will be at serious risk of eternal lostness. The Sardian Church was simply far too comfortable and compromised. In short, they were already spiritually dead and ripe for judgment. One of our greatest dangers is to look back to the 'glory days' of our churches and to rest on our past reputations. Sometimes believers need to stay on in comatosed churches and call these churches back into faithfulness and new spiritual life.

3:5 is critical. Arminians teach that apostasy can reverse the results of conversion; Calvinists claim that those who fail to persevere were never actually converted. From both angles, the end result is actually the same, namely, those who fail to persevere are lost. Some argue that those who once professed salvation but then fell away will still get to heaven. Rev 3:5 refutes this position, as do the following texts – Mk 4:16-19; John 8:30-32, 15:6; Rom 11:20-22; Gal 4:19, 5:4; 2 Peter 2:20-22. Nominal Christians must beware!

3:7-13 Philadelphia

Only Ephesus and Laodicea, out of the seven churches, fail to be specifically linked to 'Satan' in this series of letters. Jesus affirms that all churches, then and now, face the reality of spiritual warfare. It's the Church's reactions and responses that are absolutely key. Spiritual warfare is certainly *not only for the keen ones, but is also the touchstone by which our level of 'overcoming' is measured and by which we are commended or condemned by Jesus!*

We cannot escape its reality and its consequences for our churches. The Philadelphian church has "little strength" but actually has fared well in its calling to spiritual warfare. This letter underlines that Jesus 'holds the key of David'. In short, Jesus alone controls the door into the royal palace. Another way of saying this is that Jesus alone determines who can enter His household and who cannot. Many Jewish Christians were most probably expelled from their synagogues, but Jesus takes His own people into His Kingdom in the new Jerusalem. Here unbelieving Jews join unbelieving Gentiles as they bow down before the faithful believers (3:9). They have to acknowledge that God chooses His people and that He loves them. The mark of these genuine believers is that they have kept and guarded God's Word. These folk suffer temporarily on earth but their home is in heaven. The big challenge for this church is to *persevere* in their calling to warfare and the protection of the Word, lest they lose their crowns. Crowns are for overcomers, but loss of a crown means *exclusion from the kingdom* (3:5). Those who overcome will be welcome in Jesus' household but also will be *part of God's temple* (3:12). We will bear the new names of God, Temple and Jesus as new pillars of the eternal Temple. The physical Temple had been destroyed in AD 70.

The 'hour of trial' is difficult to interpret literally because it is not literal. 'Trial' more likely refers to tribulation before the end (9:15; 17:12). The phrase 'keep…from' refers to guarding God's commandments and this sole appearance in Revelation means not removal *from* trial, but protection *through* it. This text and many others show that in the Scriptures, God usually delivers His people after they are already in testing.

There is no account of Jesus' return before 19:11-16 and no reference to corporate resurrection before the 'first' resurrection in 20:4-6 at the start of the 1000 years. Jesus' followers *are* martyred right across Revelation but they are also protected from God's anger in 7:1-8. Revelation may not be referring to the 3½ or 7 year Tribulation stressed in modern prophecy teaching anyway. The believers at Philadelphia are commended for their weakness that makes them heavily dependent on God in times of Tribulation and when faith separates them from their families. Perseverance in the hope of the gospel is vital for all believers. Worship and fellowship will be key in the new Jerusalem and not just the sounds of worship but fellowship with the Person of God Himself.

3:14-22 Laodicea

Close to Colosse and Hierapolis, Laodicea was a centre for the worship of various deities and the significant Jewish community seems to have willingly blended into Greek culture in a number of ways. Jesus is very direct to this church. 'Amen' suggests the assurance of all Jesus's promises. He is faithful to all His promises (3:14) but He is also revealed here as 'first' in power and authority! The Christians no doubt shared in the self-sufficiency, wealth and material success of Laodicea but they also shared in the city's contaminated and nasty lukewarm water supply. Hot water was useful; cold likewise; but lukewarm was an embarrassment. Jesus' key complaint was that the Christians regarded themselves as self-sufficient, having uncritically absorbed the attitudes of Laodicean culture. The city boasted of its wealth as a centre for banking ; it even refused financial help for rebuilding itself, after a serious earthquake in AD 60! They also produced black cloth in quantity, so Jesus offered them 'white clothes' in contrast. Famous for various medications, Jesus offers them spiritual eye salve, ironically to help them *see their blindness* to their self-deceptions – they thought they were rich but were actually spiritually poor. Jesus urged them to buy true wealth and clothing that was *not that of this wealthy world.*

Jesus presses these strong corrections because He loves them. He wants to take control of their lives, instead of them trying to run their own lives in arrogant self-sufficiency, independently of Jesus. If the believers are ready to '*overcome*' in these ways, Jesus will share His reign with them, not only in this life, as they experience in Christ the victory over the powers of darkness, but also, and eternally, the fullness of reign with Christ once that reign is fully and finally established in the new Jerusalem. At the same time, of course, believers are subject to God. He alone is the truly divine One, not the created one. We must not try to force 'hot' to mean 'positive' and 'cold' to mean negative, in terms of our spiritual heath or sickness!

Certainly, Jesus is issuing rebukes to this church, *but this needs to be handled very carefully and sensitively in the 21st Century AD Church.* Application needs real caution to the broken, the weak, the marginalised, the suffering, the sacrificial. What Jesus is opposing is *self-satisfaction, self-security, independent pride, complacency and self-sufficiency.* He deeply desires intimacy with us as His redeemed children. He calls us to repentance that we have prized our own independence. This church in Laodicea had not felt it needed outside help, whether material or spiritual. We need to listen to the voices of other churches, especially those in the non-Western world which have suffered more deeply and more extensively than Western ones. Our relative prayer-lessness and devotional weakness exposes our real lack of sense of need before God. Wealth and comfort can lead to spiritual complacency, as can our indifference to others' suffering, persecution, injustice, poverty and oppression. Our prosperity can make us blind: we can be in love with this world, without being aware of it! Are our churches teaching biblical truth in line with Jesus' own teaching … or actually contrary to it? Jesus longs and insists to see humility, sacrifice, repentance, generosity and a spirit of willingness to reach out to the ends of the earth with biblical truth.

Summary

We have now seen something of our own vulnerability to the potential influences and impact of the World, the Flesh and the Devil.

We have also viewed how the apostle Paul in 2 Corinthians came under attack from Satan and how he dealt with such assaults.

We have also identified how Satan sought to cause damage in the seven churches of Revelation 2-3, and indeed in all subsequent churches, as he aims his evil forces to manufacture "the 10 C's" –

> Chaos, Compromise, Cowardliness, Comfort, Conflict, Control, Complacency, Confusion, Corruption, Cataracts or 'blindspots' that stop us seeing just how active Satan is in our churches.

Satan uses multiple tools of warfare to influence us and to entrap us, by interfering in our lives and ministries, with the ultimate goal of causing maximum diversion, deceit, deflection and damage in our churches. He hates God and Christ and the Church. The message of Rev 2-3 is surely, and most fundamentally, that we need to examine ourselves in our lives and ministries, to repent of all our sins, weakness and failure, and to *decide that we will take up the challenge demanded by God to 'overcome'.*

Listening to God and overcoming Satan are arguably the two key themes of the message to the seven churches in Rev 2-3 and most probably for all churches to apply now.

So, we turn to Sermons 7-10.
This Sermon 6 is intended as the transition and link between
Part 1 – how Satan works in individuals, churches and the world, and
Part 2 – how we can use divine weapons and resources to resist the Satanic Spiritual Warfare being continually played out on earth today and reflecting the warfare that has its roots in the heavenly places.

How, therefore, can we live and fight as Christians in our thoughts, attitudes, words and deeds?

We are called, equipped and saved by God.

Why?

To become the 'overcomers'.

Spiritual weapons:
7 Our Resources For Warfare

OUR ASSETS – OUR STARTING POINTS FOR ENGAGEMENT

Our position in Christ

1. Christ created the principalities and powers – Col. 1:15-17.
2. Christ has conquered the principalities and powers – Col. 2:13-15; John 12:31; Eph. 1:19b-23; 2:5-6. This victory has sealed the final doom and destiny of Satan – Mt. 8:28-29; 25:41; Mk. 1:24; Rev. 20:10.
3. Christ has redeemed us by the shedding of His blood – Col. 1:13,19-22.
4. Christ indwells and empowers us by His Spirit – Col. 1:27.
5. Christ has been raised from the dead and believers share His victory and risen life – Col. 3:1-4; Eph. 2:4-7; Rom. 8:9-11.
6. Christ's love permanently unites us with God our Father, and that bond is indissoluble and unbreakable – Col. 1:12; Rom. 8:38-39.

Our condition in Christ

1. *Committed Soldiers* – the need for a life of consecration in which we do not allow the enemy to have 'footholds' in our lives – Romans 12:1-2; 2 Tim. 2:3-7; Revelation 12:11.
2. *Cleansed Soldiers* – the need for a life of holiness, having dealt with all sin in our lives – John 8:31-32; James 1:19-27; 1 John 1:5-10.
3. *Confident Soldiers* – the need for a life of total dependence on God.
   No false confidence in human resources – 2 Cor. 10:3-5.
   Absolute confidence in the Captain of salvation – Eph.1:19-21.
   Ultimate confidence in Satan's defeat – Rev. 20:10.
   When Satan tries to remind us of our past, we can remind him of his future.

Three Abiding Principles –

a) Flee Temptation – 2 Timothy 2:2.

b) Resist Satan – James 4:7-12; 1 Peter 5:5-11.

c) Bind Satan – Matthew 12:29.

Our authority in Christ

'The Name of Jesus' This is not a magic formula, but Christ's God-given authority. It is an authority delegated to those in Christ. The 'name' encompasses Christ's Person, Christ's completed work at Calvary and Christ's continuing ministry by His Spirit for us, in us and through us – Luke 10:17-20; Acts 3:1-10; 16:16-18; Phil. 2:5-11.

Our assets in Christ

1. Knowledge of God – His Way and Will – Eph. 3:14-21.
2. Knowledge of our resources in Christ.
3. Knowledge of ourselves.
4. Knowledge of our enemy.

Our acceptance of the reality of warfare

Rick Warren, an American University Pastor, writing in January 2017, underlined that the Bible often uses certain words to describe the Christian life – fight, conquer, strive, battle, overcome, victory. He then lists six essential steps for fighting this spiritual battle –

1. Acknowledge the adversary. 1 Peter 5:8-9. Being attacked by the spiritual powers shows we are believers; it also shows we are making an impact.
2. Accept Jesus' authority. Matt 16:19. We have Christ's power and authority.
3. Put on all the armour. Eph 6:11-17. Mentally, put on truth, righteousness, gospel of peace, faith, salvation, Word of God *before you do ministry.*
4. Aim the artillery, mainly in our thought life!
5. Exercise humility and you will be more powerful in ministry. We are simply vessels in God's Hands. Expect God to work in our ministry. Exercise praise in God.
6. Avoid all distractions. We must focus ourselves. Don't take on too much in ministry. "The good can be the enemy of the best". We have only *one person* to please in this life – the Lord Jesus Christ.

Our continuing armour in Christ,

rooted in Paul's Letter to the Ephesians 6:10-20

John Abraham Godson wrote in the *Perspectives Issue* of the Lausanne World Pulse Archives in Issue, June 2009 as follows: "The Christian life is spiritual warfare.... The day we decided to become disciples of Christ we declared war against the kingdom of the devil and all his works in our lives and in our communities.... Spiritual warfare is about overcoming the enemy, his temptations, and his traps. It is about winning new territories for God".

The overall goal of the Ephesian letter: God's plan in eternity to create a single new human race through Jesus' death and resurrection. The aim is to unite church and creation under Christ's Headship. This church consists of Jews *and* Gentiles and must live a life worthy of its calling, demonstrating unity, diversity, purity and harmony. This new society was the work of God through Christ and by the Spirit and this new society was to live a transformed life by God's enabling. However, underneath this great ideal, Paul reveals an invisible force that is scheming to undermine and destroy this new society. Satan and his powers continually work to resurrect the barriers that Christ had broken down by His own death and resurrection. Paul stresses that between Christ's incarnation and His return, there will be constant conflict as Satan and his powers try to wreck God's kingdom. Christian believers are called to be involved in this warfare, and they are equipped by the Godhead to wrestle with these evil powers, employing the whole armour of God to fight as 'overcomers'.

This new society will always be the object of spiritual attack. WHY?

a) Christ has brought unity by His Spirit – Satan promotes disunity.
b) Christ has broken racial barriers – Satan builds barriers.
c) Christ has made holiness possible – Satan incites sin.

The battle is real and we are called to engagement. 'Finally' (v.10) is better translated 'henceforward' ie. for the remaining time. Conflict and struggle are actually the norm between Christ's two comings.

Ephesians 6 verses 10-12

We must know our enemy and have healthy respect for him. If the enemy were weak, we would not need the armour Christ has provided. We face cosmic, demonic forces and those who are unprepared will be battered – (Acts 19:13-17).

The spiritual forces of darkness and evil in the heavenly realms are trying to work out their evil plans here on earth. Our battle is thus not directed against human beings (See Eph 6:12). These powers may be invisible but they are definitely real and malicious in intent. In 2 Cor. 10:3-5, Paul confirms that our weapons have power to smash demonic arguments, to counter and destroy any claims that run contrary to the knowledge of God, and to bend and bring all human thoughts into obedience to the risen and reigning Christ.

These 'principalities and powers' have three features –

1. They are powerful

Kosmokratores = planets that were believed to control the fate of humans. This term was also found on inscriptions of Roman Emperors. The *Greek* implies the global, worldwide power of these powers of deep darkness, even though Christ holds the real, ultimate and overall power and authority.

2. They are evil

'World rulers of this present darkness, 'spiritual hosts of wickedness' operating 'in the heavenly places'. Wicked, dark and destructive, they have no moral principles whatsoever. It's not that their moral compass is pointing in the wrong direction; they just do not even possess a moral compass at all!

3. They are cunning

v.11 'Strategies'. Satan's method of approach is not normally as a lion roaring in an open field. He works in dark places and in unexpected ways. He prefers to encourage moral and ethical compromise and a slow drift into biblical error. He is capable of changing himself into "an angel of light", thus catching Christians off their guard by his subtle deception. Intimidation and insinuation alternate from him. Satan's masterstroke is to persuade folk that he does not even exist!

Lloyd Jones, M. The Christian Warfare, An Exposition of Eph. 6:10-13 Banner of Truth, 1976, p. 292, writes:

' I am certain that one of the main causes of the ill state of the Church today is the fact that the devil is being forgotten. All is attributed to us; we have all become so psychological in our attitude and thinking. We are ignorant of this great objective fact, the being, the existence of the devil, the adversary, the accuser, and his 'fiery darts'. '

Only *God's power* can deliver us in this battle. This power raised Christ from the dead and also raises believers from the death of sin. Christ is enthroned in the heavenly places and we share in that glorious rule. Demonic powers are working (v.12) but they *were* defeated at the Cross and are now under the feet of Christ and of ourselves. Paul's call to use the power, might and strength of Christ (v.10) employs the same three words – *dynamis, kratos and ischus* – as in Eph. 1:19, concerning God's raising of Jesus from the dead.

Verse 10 '*Be strong in the Lord and in the strength of His might.'*

- some Christians think they are strong enough not to need divine armour.
- some Christians are so self-distrustful that they feel they cannot make any contribution to warfare.

Both views are wrong. In the Christian life, *Divine Enabling* and *Human Cooperation* go together. We are to 'be strong' (present passive) and to 'put on', even though the power is God's and the armour is God's, cf. 2 Tim. 2:1; Col. 1:29. The principalities and powers (*archai* and *exousia*) against which we are called to fight, are actually *supernatural forces.* It is true that sometimes in the NT these words are used of human authorities, of structures, institutions and traditions. However, it is very clear, especially in Ephesians, that the principalities and powers are both supernatural beings and are operating in 'heavenly places'. They can of course work in and through human institutions, making use of them to fulfil their evil purposes. Let's not forget that Jesus Himself, as portrayed in the Gospels, believed in demons and angels. He was in no doubt at all.

Before we launch into a study of each element of God's spiritual armour graciously granted to us for our involvement in warfare, let's consider Iain Duguid's thought in his short 2019 book *The Whole Armor of God: How Christ's Victory Strengthens Us for Spiritual Warfare* (Crossway). He claims that perhaps the greatest success of Satan, especially across much of the Western World, has been to convince very many Christians of the non-existence and non-reality of Satan himself. Duguid states that this greatest of lies enables Satan to continue his evil work "unsuspected and undetect-ed"! Evil takes many forms in the visible, material world but the trigger – Satan – manages to work invisibly in dark places and we are deceived. Ephesians 6:12, Acts 19:18-19 and 1 Peter 5:8 make this very clear. Many in the West are so rooted in the scientific, materialist, technological world with all its benefits, that we fail to 'see' spirits.

As we enter the spiritual conflict, we need to realise afresh that the *power made available to us is the power that raised Christ from death.* God has given us *this very armour.* Our task is to realise it, wear it and use it! Only then will we fail far less often in the warfare. How exactly does this happen to us and in us? It was shown outside of us when Christ Himself resisted and overcame sin and Satan *in our place.* Then and now, it is shown inside us through the ongoing Spirit's work, who renews our hearts and minds and wills. The armour God now gives us belongs to Him, but He Himself wore that armour in the crucial battle of Christ's death and resurrection. We need to be rooted in that great victory of God over Satan and the powers of evil. We fight and stand firm against Satan only by, and in, the strength that we receive from Christ's victory won by Him for us.

Each piece of the armour *actually points us directly to Christ Himself!*

Thus, **Belt** of Truth	=	The belt that girds the messianic king (Isa. 11:5)
Breastplate of Righteousness and **Helmet** of Salvation	=	God's arsenal in Isaiah 59:17
Gospel Feet	=	The feet of those who proclaim Messiah's Kingdom in Isaiah 52:7
Shield of Faith	=	God Himself (Genesis 15)
Sword of Spirit, God's Word	=	weapon of promised servant of the Lord (Isaiah 49:2)

Jesus Himself wore this armour in His constant fight against Satan and Jesus won the victory. We are called to wear this armour of God *because this is what Jesus has already worn through His life and work, to defy and destroy Satan.* He faced the same temptations of "lust, gossip, anger, pride, self-exaltation, lying, coveting" that Jesus faced till His death. He then equipped us with the same power that raised Himself from the dead. He now raises *us* from spiritual death to new life in Christ. Each step of our spiritual regeneration and sanctification is under God's timing and control. We are not fighting this warfare against sin and Satan alone, but it does involve struggle. Phil 2:12-13 instructs us to work out our own salvation *because* God is at work in us. God will *ultimately sanctify us.* We will stand complete at the End. All progress made will be by God sanctifying us and the Holy Spirit of God will deserve the glory.

In all of this equipping for warfare, though, Duguid reminds us that God's Spirit will often leave us to ourselves and to our temptations, in order to convince us just how weak and frail we are by ourselves! He wants us to grow in humility and dependence on His grace. Spiritual failures in our lives are actually vital (Rom 7:24). Unbelievers won't struggle with temptation and sin, until the Spirit works within them.

Ephesians 6 verses 13-20, the Nature of our Divine Armour.
God is calling us to 'stand' against enemy tactics, 'withstand' in the evil day (ie. in times of severe pressure) and 'stand'. (Ephesians 6:11,13,14) A ***triple*** challenge: God calls us to **strength** and **stability** by **standing.** The goal of our putting on the divine armour is that we will be enabled to stand firm, even under the most intense and vicious Satanic assaults on our lives and ministries! Paul wants us to remain strong, stable and absolutely firm. The weapons *belong to God* but he gladly makes them available to us *for our use*!

The God who calls us also equips us. *Panoplia* = 'full armour of a heavily-armoured soldier'. In the OT God Himself was the warrior – Isa. 59:17. Today he equips us with **His Armour** so we can engage in the battle -

Belt	=	Truth
Breastplate	=	Righteousness
Boots	=	Good news of peace
Shield	=	Faith
Helmet	=	Salvation
Sword	=	Word of God

Willian Gurnall (Puritan) The Christian in Complete Armour 1655
Vol. I p.67 (1821 Ed.)
'In heaven we shall appear not in armour but in robes of glory; but here they (*sc.* the pieces of armour specified) are to be worn night and day; we must walk, work and sleep in them, or we are not true soldiers of Christ.'

The equipment available to us in Eph 6:13-20

Girdle of truth – v.14 – "having girded your loins with truth"
This was actually part of a soldier's underwear – it functioned to gather his flowing tunic together and hold his sword in place. He could thus move without restriction in the midst of battle.

Two views on the meaning –

1. The truth of doctrine as revealed in Scripture.
2. The truth in terms of honesty, sincerity and integrity of life.

Both aspects are surely needed and truth is absolutely basic to our standing against the devil. Satan hates light – he prefers to operate in darkness. Truth = the totally unique message of the Bible. What we believe about this biblical truth is supremely important. See Acts 4:12; Eph 1:13, 4:21; John 14:6.

Truth = belief in the biblical gospel message of who God is, who we are, and what He demands of us as created human beings. We must learn to understand Scripture, to believe it, to use and apply it in our lives. Believers need to be honest about themselves and ask themselves how serious they are about devoting study of Scripture. Satan will do all he can to disturb and deflect us from study, for he hates biblical truth. Satan lied from the start and we all have listened to his lies ever since... until we come face-to-face with the truth of God as it stands in Jesus Christ. God has given us His powerful Word (Ps. 19:7-11) and He loves us (Rom 8:28-31). We need to know Scripture well enough to answer demonic lies. We need a full grasp of the nature of the gospel... to address Satan!

The Messianic King was the first to show us *His Basic Righteousness and Faithfulness* to God's Word in Isaiah 11:5. Jesus followed this same pattern to deal with Satan in the Wilderness (Matt 4:4). Jesus wore this belt of the Word of Truth. We must wear this same belt, to counter Satan's efforts to lead us into wrong directions and feed our wrong appetites. Satan even attacked Jesus on the cross, but Jesus responded with His Truth. Christ's truth sets us free from the powerful bondage of Satanic lying.

Breastplate of righteousness – v. 14

This breastplate is not a list of our own achievements in life. Righteousness is not something we achieve for or by ourselves. We can never make ourselves acceptable to God. We, in and of ourselves, can never reach the moral standard that a perfectly holy God requires of us. None of us is able to overcome our sins of thought or word or deed. Rather, righteousness is a gift from God for us to wear.

A soldier's breastplate often covered his back as well as his front. This provided cover and protection for the major organs of the body. The origins of this piece of armour lie in Isaiah 59:17, around which God had promised to deal with Israel's enemy nations like Babylon. Isaiah then speaks about God's coming to deal with the greatest of His enemies, namely human sin. To achieve this, God had to put on His own armour, namely *His* breastplate of righteousness and *His* helmet of salvation. God would have needed to judge His people, but instead God intervened to deliver Israel, even though His people deserved nothing – see Isa 59:2; 64:6. The promise to Isaiah was that God would come at great personal cost, in the person of His merciful redeemer, who would win the victory by bearing the sins of His people *within Himself* in the terrible pain of the cross of Christ.

God made the sinless Christ to become sin, so that in Christ we might become the righteousness of God (2 Cor 5:21). Having righteousness means that we are justified by grace through faith in Christ crucified, we are clothed with the righteousness of Christ and we are thus totally accepted by God in the glorious gospel of Christ. At the same time, we have been equipped by God to do the good works that He has prepared for us to do (Eph 2:8-10). These are crucial lines of defence against the accusations of our 'adversary' and 'slanderer'. See Rom. 8:1,33-34. We are in a right relationship with God through Christ. This is a very strong defence against Satan's claim that we don't belong to God. *Positional* armour.

'Righteousness' can also be viewed in a moral sense by which we resist temptation – 2 Cor. 6:7; Eph. 4:24,5:9. *Truth* resists Satan's deceits and *Righteousness* resists his temptations. *Practical* armour.

These two views of righteousness are surely both necessary and inseparable. G.G.Findlay wrote, "The completeness of pardon for past offence and the integrity of character that belong to the justified life, are woven together into an impenetrable mail."

God the Father thus treated His righteous Son, Jesus, *as if he were the sinful and guilty one.* He made Jesus to be blackened and condemned with our sinful thoughts, offensive words and evil actions! On the cross, Jesus suffered spiritual separation from His Father as He paid the price for our sins (Isa 53:5,12). Utterly remarkable! God treats the innocent one as guilty and then treats the guilty ones as innocent. Duguid (2019:42) says, "Instead of counting our sins against us, God chooses to count for us Christ's righteousness…. His perfect righteousness and holy obedience are credited to our account." (2 Cor 5:19; Isa 53:5; Zechariah 3). In Christ, we have actually received a breastplate of righteousness that protects us eternally against the anger and judgment of God. This massive gift from God is available only to those who are truly and genuinely united to Christ and forgiven by Christ, through repentance and faith in Christ – see Romans 8:1; 2 Cor 5:17.

Once we have been reconciled to God through Christ and have been clothed in Christ's perfect righteousness, we have the assurance and security of God's love for us. Yet, at the same time, we are called to take sin seriously and to live as new creations in Christ, indwelt by the Holy Spirit of God who is continually at work in us to make us obedient, more like Christ in our lives and ministries. Just as a breastplate defends the key organs of a soldier, so the righteousness of Christ protects us against Satan's two main lies, namely that God doesn't actually love us and that sin doesn't actually matter. Satan loves us to wander into sin – immorality, idolatry, adultery, gay practice, theft, greed, drink, drugs, cheating, insulting. Yet Satan is continually pushed back by God as the Lord shows His superior power in the weakness of repentant but frail and feeble Christians. This means constant dependence on God and ceaseless perseverence. We must rest in the stunning power of God and not try to substitute our own righteousness for that of Christ. The righteousness we have is that given us by Christ as part of the "cosmic transfer deal by which our own guilt was laid on Jesus" (Duguid 2019:49). This is worked out in us by the Spirit, as He renews our thinking and living. We must frequently remind ourselves of the gospel and refocus on that gospel.

Gospel shoes – v. 15 – "the equipment of the gospel of peace".
Paul also expressed the verse this way: "having put on the readiness given by the gospel of peace". Warfare required adequate footwear. Again we need to take on board the OT background in Isaiah 52:7: "How beautiful upon the mountains are the feet of him who brings good news, who publishes peace, who brings good news of happiness, who publishes salvation, who says to Zion, 'Your God reigns"'.

The Roman *caliga* (half-boot) of the legionary – made of leather with free toe movement and studded soles was strapped to the ankles and shins. This boot enabled long-distance marching and prevented slipping. The 'equipment of the gospel of peace' (v.15).
'Equipment' = *hetoimasia* = 'readiness', 'preparation', 'firmness'.
Could mean two things:

> If this genitive is *subjective*, it would mean the firmness that the gospel gives to those who have embraced it. Thus we have a strong and firm foothold for our battle with the enemy.
>
> If this genitive is *objective*, it would mean our readiness to proclaim the Gospel – see Isaiah 52:7; Eph. 2:14-18; Col. 4:5-6. Duguid favours this interpretation that mainly concerns the readiness to share the gospel as heralds and to travel to do this. This idea is shared by Joel and Isaiah, in Romans 10:13-15. We are not marketing salespeople but proclaimers of God's gospel of peace to broken and oppressed people.

Satan fears and hates the liberating power of the Gospel. Even having responded to the Gospel, believers still need to hear the Gospel for their encouragement, upbuilding and evangelistic sharpening. Our calling from God is to get the gospel message right and to get it out. In Isaiah's situation, this meant your God reigns, He has redeemed Jerusalem, and the ends of the earth will see this salvation. Our gospel *is essentially the same.* In 2023, people still worship fame, celebrity, success, money. We believe this gives us identity and significance, but actually they are false gods and we easily fall into bondage to them! The gospel sets us free from such bondage and we find peace-giving power, outside of those idols.

We are to announce next that the Lord has redeemed Jerusalem and comforted His people. This points to the grace of the gospel. In early sections of Isaiah, we learn that Jerusalem had repeatedly failed – hardness, blindness and deafness to God. Such sin and failure would lead to massive divine judgment, located in Isaiah 6:9-13, but even in this condemnation, there was hope for a remnant of the people – indeed, hope ultimately for folk from many other nations as well. Jesus came to bring Jews and Gentiles together in a new body in Christ by the Spirit (Eph. 2:11-22).

Jesus Himself was the first to wear these shoes *in our place*. Thus He came as a herald but also the One who died for our sins to turn believers from being enemies of God into friends of God, by repentance and faith. This brought us peace with God. See Isaiah 61 where Jesus is prophesied as the Spirit-filled servant of the Lord, anointed by God to proclaim good news, liberty and the year of the Lord's favour. He will comfort the mourners (Luke 4:18-19). Jesus was indeed the perfect-pattern evangelist! (See John 4:1-26; Lk 5:12-13; Mark 5:22-42, by which Jesus became our peace). We have peace with God through the gospel which brought us into God's own family. We ourselves need this peace as we confess sin and rebellion against Him, turning our eyes and attention from self to Saviour. The prophet Isaiah looked to God and felt dirty to the core (Isaiah 6:1-7). An angel was sent by God not to condemn him but to cleanse him! Isaiah felt the redemption and hope he was called to proclaim to others! He then knew he was the one to announce God's peace to others (6:8). It would be a tough road for Isaiah – and will be ultimately for us – but this gospel of peace will equip us with endurance and perseverance, right to the very End, when the warfare will finally be complete in glory!

In the meantime, this God of peace will still be at work even when we ourselves despair at our own evangelistic apathy. God is not defeated. He will complete His work of global mission. Jesus worked with incompetent and stubborn disciples among hostile Jewish audiences. Jesus lived life at God's pace, simply doing the works of God each day, whilst enjoying that peace that He had with God and that He gives us.

Shield of faith – v. 16 – against "all the flaming darts of the evil one". The *scutum* was the long oblong shield (1.2 metres x 0.75 metre) that covered the whole person and was made from wood, hide and iron. This shield gave protection against flaming missiles. The demonic darts could be evil accusations and false guilt, also suggestions and thoughts made by Satan, trying to instill, into our Christian minds, doubts, disobedience, rebellion, fears, lusts, anger and evil plans.

By faith we can flee to God for refuge, since He Himself is our shield. When doubt and depression come, faith takes on board God's promises. When temptation threatens to overwhelm us, faith opens up God's power. The key question, however, must be what is the foundation of this faith. Thus, faith in Christ's resurrection only carries meaning if it is actually true. The object of our faith is the vital factor. Faith itself is the instrument that links us to the mighty, powerful and trustworthy God. Thus, can Paul write "In all circumstances take up the shield of faith, with which you can extinguish all the flaming darts of the evil one" (Eph 6:16). What he means is that faith protects us from Satan's attacks because of that which faith connects us to, namely the power and protection of our mighty God Himself.

The OT contains many references, not to faith *per se*, but to the God who is our shield. See Genesis 15:1; Prov. 30:5; Psalm 3:3, 28:7, 119:114. Psalm 91:3-6 carries the context of assaults on the writer. Paul tells us that faith is the mechanism by which we flee to God and find refuge in Him. Faith is not merely belief in God; it means that God is our trustworthy rope of salvation when we actually grab that rope and are pulled to safety in Christ. We have to *know that God has the power to pull us in, as it were, and deliver us.* He is sovereign over every detail of cosmos and human lives! We need to hold onto this when the evil powers around us seem rampant and the world appears to be spinning headlong out of control! God is powerful but He is also our constant ally – see Psalm 77. He is utterly on our side!

Our faith must be built on unchangeable biblical truth as it is revealed in God's Word. The Scriptures are incredibly honest about the fallen, corrupted nature of human beings in deep rebellion against God. We are by nature desperately lost and estranged from the true God in the sins of thought, word and deed. There is no reason whatsoever why God should even think of rescuing us. Yet, God stepped in and brought us out of darkness into light (Eph 2:4). He took the initiative to reach out to us while we were 'drowning'...to prove to us that He was and is truly on our side! He did this by that great gospel exchange: God the Father treated His Son Jesus, the only innocent person on the planet, as if He were guilty, so that He could treat us, the guilty, as though we were innocent. The Father punished our sin in His innocent Son during Christ's horrendous mental, physical and spiritual suffering endured on the cross. Our repentance and faith in God gave us forgiveness, righteousness and reconciliation.

Our faith leads us to realise God's promises to all His people. He has planned a glorious eternity for all His children and this makes us "sure of what we hope for and certain of what we don't see" (Hebrews 11:1). Even our greatest struggles in this life will one day seem like very light and temporary afflictions by comparison. We need to recall these promises, especially when we walk in deepest darkness – see Ps 23:4; Rom 8:38. God restricts the pain He allows us to endure, for the sake of our growth and sanctification. These great truths and promises enable faith to grasp hold of the power of this God. This faith equips us to believe that God is more than able to fight Satan on our behalf in all his efforts to crush us in our own weakness (1 John 4:4). We cast ourselves on God in the battles and plead for *His strength, for His wisdom, for His clarity, for His direction, for God's words for someone, for His power and His love.*

Yet, amidst these glorious truths, there will be times when we struggle really to confess God's utter sovereignty and goodness. Yes, there will! We cry out, "I believe; Lord, help my unbelief!". Ultimately, it is not our faith that protects us, but God Himself. Jesus prays for us, that our faith may not fail (Luke 22:31-32). Jesus protected Peter's faith – and ourselves too – in the midst of Peter's sifting by Satan! Faith trusts in the love, power and goodness of the living God. He is the Shield who will extinguish Satan's flaming darts. God's faithfulness is the Shield that ensures our spiritual safety always.

Helmet of salvation – v. 17

Made of bronze or iron, with inner felt or sponge lining for ease of wear. God's saving power is our hope and our defence against the enemy –

1. *Already received:* forgiveness, deliverance from enemy bondage, adoption into the family of God. Could signify the protection of a believer's head – the source of our thoughts that will be a key target for Satan's repeated assaults and daily insinuations.
2. *Not yet fully received:* resurrection glory and complete conformity to Christ in heaven.

A soldier is unlikely to forget to wear shoes, but might possible forget to don a helmet. This helmet of salvation is drawn from Isaiah 59:17 and Isaiah makes frequent connections between righteousness and salvation eg. Isaiah 57:5-8. Thus God's righteousness refers to His cast-iron assurance to carry out all His promises to His people. He thus guarantees to deliver us from all our enemies, especially from our own sin. We have this great *hope*, which Paul describes as "*the hope of salvation*" (1 Thess. 5:8). But what is this hope of salvation? Unlike a thin and floppy sun hat – a vague optimism for serious warfare – biblical hope is a settled conviction and assurance that Christians will be eternally saved (1 Peter 3:15). That assurance does not depend on our own goodness or efforts. Rather is it rooted in the gift of God, namely Christ…*if He dwells in us by His Spirit* (1 John 5:11-12). God's righteousness and our sure hope of salvation are actually linked together in our Christian lives, as in the Book of Isaiah itself. It is not arrogance to believe we are heading for glory: it is God's gift. Yet again, we see Christ as the One who has donned the armour of God, this time in Isaiah 59:17, recording the Lord's wearing of righteousness as his breastplate and the helmet of salvation on his head… a perfect life and a perfect hope, even in Christ's darkest days. See also Hebrews 5:8,9; 12:2. Our salvation has already been won for us by Christ; its full consummation awaits the new heaven and earth.

The helmet protects us from shocks, punches and bullets, especially in times of danger and dire circumstances and when we are pressed by the enemy towards discouragement or even deep despair. God is always in control, using our afflictions to yield perseverance and character, in preparation for our entry to life in the final glory. Meanwhile hope sustains in sicknesses, failures, struggles, and anxieties about finances, future and fears. Hope also helps us to continue to battle against our ongoing sinful ways (Romans 6:14). God *will* finally bring us to completion. Our crucial hope lies firmly in the sovereign and perfect hope of God. We cling to that at all times and think constantly about the gospel, our forgiveness and our hope of heaven with the reigning and ruling Christ Jesus Himself. Always remember that He began the good work in us – and will complete it.

Sword of the Spirit – v. 17

The only one of the six that is both defensive and offensive. This is the short, close-combat sword – *machaira.* This is the *Word Of God*, seen also in Rev. 1:16; 2:12; 19:15 as proceeding from the mouth of Christ. Thus, this sword might also involve words that Christ might give us by the Holy Spirit in the heat of the battle, eg. during trials, suffering and persecution – Matt. 10:17-20.

God still uses His Word to cut through people's defences, awaken their consciences and bring them to life. This sword is 'sharper than any two-edged sword'. It is ultimately *Divine Truth* that transforms human beings, in the contexts of evangelism, temptation, counselling, teaching, preaching and spiritual growth to maturity. This divine truth does indeed project Word, Cross and Gospel into human lives to bring about life-changing and life-lasting transformation in people. This of course includes – even begins with – ourselves in our personal battle to beat our temptations and grow in holiness and fruitfulness of Christian life. We must use *every element of our weaponry* because our enemy, Satan and his evil powers, is working from every possible angle to attack and overcome us! We must overcome him by every effort. We need to know, understand and apply God's Word into our lives.

Thus far the weapons we have examined have been defensive *but the sword of the Spirit – the Bible – is highly offensive, for the pulling down of demonic forces.* Jesus Himself used this Word to deal with Satanic attacks, recorded in Matt 4, in which Jesus faced three temptations. Verse 3 mirrors Israel's moaning about lack of food; verse 6 mirrors Israel's temptation to put the Lord to the test; verse 9 mirrors Israel's temptation to false worship. Jesus realised the *ends* were not wrong, but the Satanic *means* clearly *were wrong.*

Jesus answers Satan with Scripture – Deut 8:3; Deut 6:16; Deut 6:13. These powerful Words of God sent Satan scurrying! We tend to meet sinful temptations with reasoned arguments, like 'Will I get caught?' Satan wins the day! We need to address Satan with words of Scripture, to drive him away. We must study the Word as often as we possibly can. This Word is *very powerful* because it is actually and ultimately authored by our God.

This sword is also a pair of shears with which God prunes the dross out of our lives and a scalpel by which He operates on our heart. God sees all things, all of the time. The Word convicts us of sin, self-righteousness, personal pride. We need the perfect righteousness of Christ instead. Jesus exercised this sword as a Judge (Isa 49:2,4) against nations, but was rejected and humiliated. Jesus had to be deeply wounded before He could be raised ready for His powerful use of the Word in our lives by His Spirit. ***He** is the Word and He wields that Word.*

This radical and saving change in lives is our ultimate goal for the global gospel mission that seeks to glorify God, and these weapons of spiritual warfare operate simultaneously and continually by the power of *Prayer and Spirit,* to which issues we now turn for our consideration, comprehension and application to life and ministry.

Spiritual weapons:
8 The Place of Persistent Prayer in Spiritual Warfare

As we prepare to enter a time of prayer, it will surely be valuable to remind ourselves of the tremendous truths of Paul's Letter to the Colossians, 2:6-15, in which the apostle presses the believers to continue and persevere in the faith. The truth is that doctrine and behaviour, theology and ethics always go together. How? By walking in Christ, rooted, built up and established in Him, with great gratitude. Paul warns them not to be easily deceived by Satan's aides and workers. By contrast, they must continue in the Christ who has filled them and who rules all things (2:10). We have died to sin; we have been buried with Him in baptism; we have been raised from the dead with Him by faith in God's power; we have been made alive with Him. Notice the passive voices of the verbs here: believers, filled with Christ, are linked inextricably with Christ's death, burial and resurrection. This describes the end of their old lives and the start and continuation of their new lives in Christ. God is continually at work in the lives of His disciples. It is so easy to forget that! Christ can deal with the threats that come from false teachers. Why? Because He knows that behind false teachers lie the forces of evil and darkness that He has already overcome by His death, resurrection and exaltation. The crux of all this section is that Christ has forgiven all His repentant and believing disciples, both then and now! (2:13). We have been set free from Satan's kingdom of darkness and deceit and brought into the life and light of the Kingdom of Christ.

Paul here refers to those still outside of Christ and separated from Him by their sin, disobedience and rebellion. Now, in Christ, the cause of spiritual death has been taken away. God has removed the impossible debt to God that we were trapped in because of our sin and sinful nature. God had even destroyed the document on which the debt had been recorded as an IOU evidence of the obligation to God that we could never in a million years have paid back to God! Jews had agreed to obey the law but their breaking of that contract meant death for them eternally. Gentiles, meanwhile, were bound to a similar obligation to keep what they dimly saw as the moral law, but they too had failed to do this. Both groups were doomed by their failures to follow the accompanying regulations! The debt was simply impossible to pay. But, incredibly, God had stepped in to pay this debt. He had wiped it out and cancelled it. How? By nailing it to the cross! Our debt has been totally forgiven because Christ had been nailed to the cross.

Col 2:15 stresses that those who still feared, and today still do fear, dark and evil supernatural powers, now have a message of real and genuine hope. The message is simply this – that, even though Satan has held us in his grip and bondage, God has defeated and disarmed the evil powers and has stripped away their authority. Indeed God has made of them a public spectacle, exposing them as defeated and helpless, and they are now being led by Christ in His triumphal procession. Why? So that the world/globe/ cosmos might view the sheer greatness and majesty of the stunning greatness of Christ, by His death, resurrection and exaltation to His, and His disciples', eternal victory!

Eph. 6:18-20 – Prayer needs to accompany and saturate all our spiritual warfare in life and ministry and outreach to others. The prayer we offer is a recognition of our utter dependence on God in warfare, for it is to be exercised in the Spirit. That prayer is triggered and guided by the Spirit of God. His joint gifts to us for our use are Scripture and prayer. We are to pray constantly, regularly, variously, perseveringly and for the unity of God's new society, the Church. We need to be awake and alert, always ready for the unexpected, including the Lord's Return and the suddenness of Satan's attacks. Prayer renews our strength. In verse 19, Paul admits his own great need for prayer. He needed strength and humility, as well as prayer for his energy and equipping in evangelistic work. He "welcomed all who came to him"! He did that openly and unhindered! Paul asks prayer for the freedom to preach, for boldness, for courage, for clarity, for simplicity. He calls the gospel the mystery, for it came by revelation and it brought together Jew and Gentile. These are all gifts of God. Verse 20 tells us that he was imprisoned. Why? Because of the gospel, the Lord and the Gentiles. These three are interconnected and he paid the price of his freedom for the three! Prayer would see him through and it is this sort of persevering prayer that renders the principalities and powers weak and helpless.

John Godson (2009) wrote crucially that "The reason why spiritual warfare is so important is that prayer is not only about talking to God; it is also about defeating the devil and his evil plans. However, we may not be conscious of the spiritual activity going on around us and in our communities and nations. We participate in this warfare through our prayers and witness". Godson then relates the passage from Daniel 10:2-13 in which the prophet Daniel had been mourning, fasting and praying over a period of three weeks. He was earnestly seeking the face of the Lord but no response seemed to be coming, but on the 21st day, an angel came with the explanation that the prince of Persia had resisted the angel and delayed him. Actually, God had granted an answer to Daniel from the first day and moment he began to pray! However, the answer did not reach him until Michael came to assist the angel to fight the prince of Persia who was in fact the demonic prince over the kingdom of Persia. The truth and reality of this series of events teaches us that prayer and persistence are inseparable. Satan is determined to wreck God's work on earth by ruining all that we seek to do for the glorious kingdom of God, yet we as disciples are the winners in the spiritual warfare here on the earth.

We need to learn the vital lesson that we cannot bring human beings into God's kingdom by reasoning or coercing or compelling them. It is our persevering prayer that unleashes divine powers, as angels are enlisted to fight for us (See Mark 3:27 and Matt 11:12; 18:18). We need to reflect on our God-given power to set out, to fight and to persevere – see James 4:7; 1 Peter 5:8-9; Luke 10:19. Yet again, the Scriptures promise to equip us to be overcomers in the warfare. Very helpfully, *Matt Erickson,* writing in Home Life Magazine June 2016, reminds us that "Prayer activates all of the rest of the spiritual armour….Prayer is the divinely authorised mechanism God has given us to tap into His power. Without prayer, we'll be ineffective in spiritual warfare. But with it, we will be victorious". (Quoted from *Priscilla Shirer's* latest Bible Study on the Armour of God.)

Shirer is convinced that people seem to be prone to viewing their problems and battles in "non-spiritual terms", with the result that they tend to look for "non-spiritual solutions". She expands her thinking as follows – "Everything that occurs in the visible, physical world is directly connected to the wrestling match being waged in the invisible, spiritual world. The effects of the war going on in the unseen world reveal themselves in our strained and damaged relationships, emotional instability, mental fatigue, physical exhaustion and many other areas of life. Many of us feel pinned down by anger, unforgiveness, pride, comparisons, insecurity, discord, fear… and the list goes on. But the overarching, primary nemesis behind all these outcomes is the devil himself". (see Eph 6:12) The Christian response should be to have and to seek more and more awareness, vision and insight into our true position in Christ and into a realisation that we have been given all the spiritual weapons we need to be victorious overcomers. We need the spiritual eyes to see this truth. We need to pray for divine help in the spiritual warfare.

Shirer rightly points out that Satan's assaults are wrapped up in lying deception that seeks to distort the truth about our God and about ourselves. Satan prods us into sin and a failure to trust God, especially whenever we are at our weakest and most vulnerable. Satan wants us to fall, to fail and to flounder as believing and practising disciples of Christ. Satan is cunning rather than clever! We need to be serious, open and honest with God in our prayer, but never lose sight of the truth that God is continually directing and controlling the circumstances of our lives. As Shirer declares, "Prayer is how we see heaven invade earth. It's what opens up the floodgates for God to come down and to be involved in our everyday circumstances".

***Jerry Bridges*,** writing in 1984, in Discipleship Journal Issue 19, explains a number of key issues regarding the centrality of prayer. He sets his work in 2 Kings 3 where Joram king of Israel launches battle against the king of Moab, but without seeking the face of God for this initiative. Joram then got assistance from Jehoshaphat, King of Judah and then more help from the king of Edom. This alliance soon hit problems of water supply in the desert and this forced the alliance to start praying. God spoke to the prophet Elisha and the water was eventually supplied by God. Many Christians only really get praying when they hit a particular, felt need. That often means they fail to pray for the really important and strategic issues that scream out for our prayers. The huge need to pray for labourers to enter global mission fields will often be swamped by a myriad of much smaller and 'immediate' felt needs. The really important gets squeezed out. Bridges names three levels of prayer – *Strategic* = the ultimate objective *ie.* to defeat the enemy and to bring Satan into submission; *Tactical* = the specific battles needed to achieve the ultimate goal; *Logistical* = the supply of the physical needs of the army engaged in the battle. Bridges then claims that 75%-80% of our prayers are for logistical needs of people in our churches. Important, yes, but not really strategic. He then argues that 15%-20% of our prayers are tactical eg. a conference on Evangelism, but not actually prayer for new workers! Finally, he maintains that little of our prayer effort is actually strategic ie. centred on the spiritual battle that God wants us to focus on.

Bridges suggests that we need to go through four stages of thought and action regarding spiritual warfare:

1. **U**nderstanding Satan and his evil angels – The devil rules a kingdom in which all unsaved people are held in bondage and blindness. We all lived in sin – Eph 2:1-2 – as members of this kingdom of darkness. Satan stealthily but successfully holds such folk in their spiritual blindness of the mind. They are thus unable to see the light of the gospel – 2 Cor 4:4. We must bind the powers of darkness by prayer – Matt 12:29. This witness that we give to unbelievers will be strongly opposed by Satan and his forces. He will attack us by turning himself into an 'angel of light' (2 Cor 11:14), seeking to persuade us that his

false teaching is actually the truth! See 2 Timothy 2:22-26. Satan, however, is a defeated enemy – Colossians 2:14-15. Because of Christ's victory at the Cross and Empty Tomb, we are invited in James 4:7 to resist Satan and he will flee!

2. **U**sing the correct weapons – We do not use human logic or skill, but rather, as 2 Cor 10:3-5 says, we fight Satan for human minds, using divine truth as our weapon. We are to use the biblical truth of Scripture, presented in our witness by prayer in the Spirit. That is how God transforms human beings!

3. **U**nderstanding the nature of the warfare we are in – We are fighting against an enemy that is both invisible and powerful. It is indeed a fight and struggle, and Paul stresses this in Colossians 1:28-29, where he writes, 'I *agonise* in the ministry of the word'. This brought Paul, and still brings all serious Christians, into the heat of spiritual warfare in their experience of intense fighting. Col 4:12 Paul encourages Epaphras to continue his wrestling in prayer that believers will stand firm. He wanted people to grow in Christ; *that* is strategic praying!

4. **U**ltimate goal must be our focus – Crucial for our strategic praying is for people to see the love of God in Christ's death and resurrection and to be changed by it. Rooted in Genesis 12:3 we pray that people are blessed through Abraham and his descendants. We should be praying for this. Yes, we should pray for the tactical and logistical issues – though 'these are light things in the eyes of the Lord' – but our deep concern should be to pray strategically – for the Lord to send workers into the spiritual harvest fields of the globe. Expect fruit!

Mark Bubeck notes in his work on 'Overcoming the Adversary' in his contribution to Moody Bible Institute, Chicago, 1984, that "None of us will be successful in spiritual warfare without prayer". In Eph 1:15-23, Paul prays that God will reveal to the Ephesian believers "what they already have", namely the glorious riches available to all who are in Christ. Prayer is crucial in enlightening and enabling us actually to enjoy these glorious riches of God in Christ. Bubeck emphasises that every great success and triumph of God in His work on earth has been preceded and heralded by hard, persistent prayer! These prayers will be many and varied in nature. Especially important is the need to praise God in our prayers, for this sustained praise will be effective in rebuking demonic afflictions in people. Our weapons, especially the weapon of prayer, will indeed demolish demonic strongholds (2 Cor 10:3-4). Joshua and the people of Israel won a great victory against the solidly defended city of Jericho. However, prayer and obedience to God's Word caused the walls to fall in that great victory of spiritual warfare. We can defeat Satan by prayer and plunder his 'possessions and power' in order to do God's Will.

We are called by Paul to pray in the Spirit but this needs to include a testing of the spirits as in 1 John 4:1-4, especially if we are seeking to pray in tongues. We need to ask the spirit, says Bubeck, such questions as "Has Jesus Christ come in the flesh? Is Jesus Christ Lord? Do you honour the blood of Jesus Christ?" The true Holy Spirit always witnesses in us the answer 'Yes' to such questions. Praying in the Spirit means praying in harmony with the Spirit or under the control of the Spirit. We are promised these very things as we ask the Spirit's help (Romans 8:26-27). We need constantly to heed the warning of James 4:3: "When you ask, you do not receive, because you ask with wrong motives, that you may spend what you get on your pleasures". Clearly we need to pray in harmony with the truth of God's Word (2 Timothy 3:16-17). Praying God's Word back to Him, as it were, ensures that we are in line with God's Will eg. Eph 3:14-21; Matt 6:9-13. Don't let the warmth or coldness of our *feelings* in prayer be the measure of our effectiveness in prayer. Many prayers in the Psalms were born out of sheer misery and agony, like Psalms 28, 55, 102.

Paul in Ephesians calls believers to be alert as they engage in spiritual warfare. Beware of surprise attack from unseen enemies. Pray for protection for our lives, ministries, families, friends and churches. Jesus prayed protection for Peter (Luke 22:31-32). See also John 17. Be aware that Satan is sometimes allowed the opportunity to afflict us with illness, misfortune or misery. We ask for protection from God in our 'warfare praying'. God is able to protect us as our sovereign protecting Shepherd, with armies of guardian angels.

Perseverance and persistence in prayer are needed all the time, even when things seem to be going well. Our personal holiness needs to be covered in warfare prayer – we must be open and honest with God; we need to recognise that we are dead with Christ to the rule and reign of sin (Rom 6:11); that we are not to let sin rule in our bodies (Rom 6:12), that we have been crucified with Christ (Gal 2:20), that we need the Holy Spirit to replace our sinful desires with holy desires (Gal 5: 22-23). As Christian disciples, we need to insist on putting this sequence of actions into practice. In Acts 16, Paul and Silas, in prison for casting a demon from a fortune-teller, insisted and persisted in praying and singing until the prison shook and they were free! Evil absolutely must yield to biblical truth. Our first and primary responsibility for warfare praying is for ourselves, for our lives and ministries. Then we need to prioritise our family, church, denomination, overseas workers and the global Body of Christ. Ask God to burden you with a longing to pray for one particular nation or people group. Paul asks the Ephesian believers to pray that he will have greater ability to communicate the gospel. Satan will always try to stifle the powerful communication of the gospel to a lost world. Alongside such prayer, we long for courage and boldness in our preaching and teaching, but we must also pray for open ears and receptive hearts. It helps greatly to lessen or remove spiritual blindness or deafness that Satan uses to prevent real conversions. There are truly no bounds to the global power and effect of prayer.

It is a healthy and sobering fact that in our use of the six weapons within the context of prayer, we are totally dependent on God and even our prayer is prompted and controlled by the Holy Spirit.

A few brief practical thoughts on prayer from the NT –

a) Jesus Himself gave strong emphasis on the need for watchfulness in prayer, eg's. Mk 13:33ff, 14:34-38; Lk 12:37ff; Acts 20:31; 1 Cor16:13; Col 4:2; 1 Thess. 5:1-8; 1 Peter 5:8; Rev. 3:2-3, 16:15.
b) All of us in Christian life and ministry, with their challenge of spiritual warfare, need to gather together a group of prayer supporters – see Eph 6:19; Acts 26:18; 28:17,23-24,30-31.
c) Eph 6:19-20 indicates our specific need in prayer – that we might communicate with clarity and with courage. It was said of Martin Luther by friend and foe alike: 'It is impossible to misunderstand him'.
d) The Apostle Paul was not concerned to be set free from his prison chains but rather that the Word of the Gospel might be set free to fulfill the purposes of God, which includes the submission of all things and all people to Christ, as well as the final destruction of Satan himself.
e) Prayer really is the means or mechanism by which we engage the Spirit's power whenever we use the Word. Prayer and Spirit work together, as we use God's Word to deal with the spiritual and material matters and challenges of this life.

Very significantly, Duguid points out that "It is not enough simply to put on the armour. There will be no powerful reality to your walk with God unless you are in intimate contact with your heavenly Father." (2019:103) Prayer is the key to the effectiveness of all the weaponry and to divine control and guidance of the warfare. So often prayer can become the last thing on our minds. That's the tragedy! Prayer arises when we are in total dependence on God Himself.

We looked at prayer earlier in this sermon but let's return once more to **Eph 6:18-20** to draw out some further important thoughts –

a) We don't pray simply to be seen by others or to squeeze selfishly from God the things we personally desire for ourselves (James 4:2-3). Prayer needs to emerge from our relationship with God and His Word. Our prayer must be triggered and guided by the Holy Spirit. So, praying in the Spirit is done by God's own children (John 1:12; Rom 8:14-16). The Spirit in us gives us the confidence and ability to pray to our Father. That was simply not always the case. It took Jesus' death for sin and resurrection to new life that made us His children. Praying to God is both highly personal and highly relational in Christ.

b) We don't despair or drift away from faith, if God does not give us the response to the genuine things we pray for. Duguid reminds us that we are in an ongoing relationship with God and sometimes that means painful, sad and difficult lessons need to be learned. God's power and strength is made mature and perfect in us when it is shown in our own great weakness. We grow in faith and trust by our sickness, our unemployment, our bereavement, our brokenness, our loneliness. After all, God's Spirit was with Paul in prison as he wrote the words of this Ephesian Letter - for Paul's good and Christ's own glory. He trains us in holiness and righteousness.

c) We don't give up praying at certain times and seasons (James 5:13-14). We need to share with God our sorrows and our joys. That's what we want our children to do with us as parents – to tell us everything. We need to share our thoughts and feelings with our Father as and when they happen throughout the day. We need to ask for big things, as well as small ones. God actually does choose to be at work in response to our prayers. Pray for small details but also for church unity. Pray for our own growth in holiness and for that of others. Pray for Christian workers, preachers, teachers and trainers. Pray for family, church and community. Prayer means responding to the triggers and prompts of the Spirit. This should really lighten the felt load of praying. We are not alone in our praying. The Spirit leads in our praying; we simply follow His lead. Read and study John 17. Jesus is even now praying for us: see Hebrews 7:25 and Romans 8:26. His constant intercession for us ensures that we are praying along Spirit-led ways that are the best for us. God will give us peace not to fear even the most challenging battles.

Spiritual weapons:
9 The Power of the Holy Spirit in Spiritual Warfare

The spiritual realm precedes, affects and in many ways decides what happens in the physical realm of life. Yet, herein lies a real challenge for people in the Western world in particular. Why? We live in a highly materialistic world which easily conceals and camouflages the spiritual world, rendering the latter relatively unreal and unimportant! If we fail to tackle the *spiritual* causes of our personal, social and communal problems, then we will often become confused, bewildered and ineffective, especially in our Christian lives and ministries. In a nutshell, this lack of focus on the third person of the Trinity has blurred our understanding of the Spirit's key task to make real in our experience the reality and life of Jesus Christ. The death and resurrection of Christ need to be paralleled in our own lives as we die to sin, self and Satan, whilst living out the resurrection life of Christ. All of this transformation and equipping is made possible by the work of the Holy Spirit constantly at work within our minds, hearts and wills, as He lives out the life of the Christ who indwells us. Let's examine in more detail just how the Spirit enables us in warfare.

The Spirit indwells Christian believers – We need to be aware that the Spirit of the living God lives in us as Christ's disciples (John 14:17) and that this Holy Spirit within us is indeed greater than Satan and his demonic forces that live in the world to oppose Christ and His Church in their ongoing spiritual warfare against us. Paul in Galatians 5:17 explains that we still have sinful natures and desires that work against God's purposes, priorities and plans. Spirit and flesh are engaged in an ongoing battle with each other to control our life directions. The Holy Spirit, however, is a Person with Power, not a vague spiritual force, and the Holy Spirit *fights for us*! He enables us to do amazing things as Christians, for His Spirit within us is indeed far greater than all the opposition we will ever face in the warfare. Satan and his demons currently control this dark and hostile world, but we are victorious, because no demon can withstand the presence and power of God, the Christ and the Holy Spirit. This is the situation.

The Spirit gives us discernment and understanding of Warfare – We need to be equipped to discern and distinguish between godly and evil spirits. This ability is given to us by the Holy Spirit (1 Cor 12:10), who enables us to defeat ideas and philosophies that are not actually from God (2 Cor 10:3-5). Remarkably, the Spirit knows God's thoughts *and* our thoughts. Crucially that same Spirit has *wisdom for us that is unavailable anywhere else*! Such wisdom enables us to win spiritual battles (1 Cor 2:10-13). The

Spirit knows and shows wisdom that we don't possess. He knows when we are weak in the midst of warfare, needing comfort, encouragement and uplift. Indeed, the Spirit draws close by us to give grace to persevere even in the most draining of spiritual battles, as we fight against evil spirits, temptation, sin and deep despondency. The Spirit actually works and testifies with our own spirit that we truly and really are children of God (Rom 8:16-17), having names that are sealed in the glory of heaven and identities that prove we belong eternally to the living God. Our responsibility is to ask God to allow the Spirit to strengthen us in His spiritual armour, so that we are not left exposed or vulnerable at all to the attacks of demonic forces.

The Spirit guides and empowers us into holiness of life – Rom 6:1-4 affirms that we are free from temptation and from previous bodily desires, but Eph 2:1-5 tells us that the Spirit helps us to remain *dead to sin* and to defend ourselves against temptation and desire. We have been set free by the Holy Spirit to fight spiritual battles as free warriors. Indeed, when temptation knocks on our doors, we have already bolted and locked those doors. The Spirit grants us courage and boldness to choose ways of escape from the temptations (1 Cor 10:31). Satan will always be looking for ways to entice us back into temptation and sin, so as to distract us from the holiness battle. Nominal Christians will be especially vulnerable to such traps. Satan constantly plays tricks to stumble us and to divert us from the Spirit's Work in ourselves and our churches. It is the Spirit, though, who keeps us conscious and attentive to the spiritual battles being fought around us and within us. He keeps the war zone on our screens of awareness and reminds us of the many and varied tactics of our enemy. Indeed, the Spirit keeps us walking the pathways of holiness. Walk in Him!

The Spirit teaches us truth and leads us constantly into it. Indeed He keeps us in that truth – Spirit and Word operate together powerfully and decisively in human lives. Our responsibility is to employ Scripture, to pray and to give our testimony to Christ in our lives. It is exclusively the work of the Spirit to enlighten and enliven unbelievers into the kingdom of the living Christ. This 'Trinity' of Prayer, Spirit and Word is more than enough to defeat all the efforts of the enemy to crush evangelism and church growth. The Kingdom of God cannot be brushed aside. How does this work of the Spirit operate in actual practice?

The trinity of the Godhead has already defeated and condemned Satan, the temporary ruler of this world (John 16:8). The Spirit both convicts the world of sin and indwells all who turn to Christ in true repentance and faith (John 16:7,11).

The Holy Spirit is the 'hidden' source of our power because He is the Spirit of Truth (John 14:17; 15:26; 16:13; 1 John 4:6). The Spirit, working with the Word, works secretly but stunningly, to enable us to see the difference between truth and error. As we have already seen, one of Satan's main weapons is lying, half lying and twisting the truth in subtle ways (John 8:44). He loves to point the finger at us concerning our sins (Rev 12:10). We do need to recognise that he has a degree of power as he tries to destroy and devour us (1 Peter 5:8). Many are easily deceived by him, but the power of the Spirit equips us to resist his arrows.

The world doesn't know or understand the Spirit. The world, Satan and his demons cannot understand the things of the Spirit (1 Cor 2:14-16; John 14:16-17). Believers have spiritual insight and understanding because we are indwelt by the Spirit. The Spirit leads us into all truth in order to protect us from the multiple deceptions of the enemy. The Spirit also leads us into holiness of life so that we are equipped to resist the temptations and desires of our previous life of the flesh. The Holy Spirit within us is indeed far greater than any evil spirits we may face in the warfare.

The truth of God's Word – the "belt of truth" – will indeed protect us from false accusations and suggestions from the powers of darkness. We will be attacked from the three dimensional world, flesh and devil as we seek to advance the kingdom of Christ and His righteousness. Our duty is to allow the Lord to plant His Word into us richly and deeply. Then we will not be fearful, uncertain or doubtful about the promises of God. The belt of truth is defensive, but alongside that function, the Holy Spirit uses the powerful, offensive impact of the Word of God. Thus, we need to become more and more effective in our use of Scripture to impart to ourselves and others the wisdom, power, knowledge and persuasion of biblical truth.

The Holy Spirit functions in even more ways than we may sometimes be aware of. Thus, the Spirit gifts and credits the righteousness of Christ *to our bank account* even though we don't actually deserve that righteousness in any way. This gift of Christ's own righteousness then works within us to enable us to carry out practical acts of righteousness. The Spirit produces in us the fruit of the Spirit (Gal 5:16-26). This is the work of our breastplate of righteousness (Eph 6:14b). The Holy Spirit also empowers us to preach, teach and share the gospel of Christ, including personal witness. This is our "ready feet" from our gospel of peace (Eph. 6:15). This gospel needs to be presented *with the power of the Spirit* so as to deliver inspiration, information and sincere persuasion. According to Eph 6:16, we absolutely do need the

Holy Spirit to deflect the enemy's evil darts. As we see the power of the Holy Spirit at work, so our faith is strengthened in ways that far exceed our own human strength and wisdom. We are enabled to live and work in ways, and at levels, that defy mere human explanation! This sheer power of God is inseparable from "taking the helmet of salvation" (Eph 6:17), by which we experience the strength and deep assurance of our salvation, even in the midst of the most horrifying challenges that shake us up.

The Holy Spirit intervenes even, indeed especially, in our praying. He clears the way, aids our focus and acts as megaphone to our heavenly Father (Eph 6:18). Praying in the Spirit means that we are actually being led, taught and moved in prayer. Our constant need is to ask the Spirit to help us to pray in the Spirit, with a whole range of praise, confession, thankfulness and requests. We really do need to build around us a circle of prayer supporters *who will faithfully pray with us and for us in our lives and ministries.*

The Holy Spirit makes provision in spiritual warfare not just by giving the weapons to defend against every attack and to move forward the kingdom of God, but He also provides the praying support army whose encouragement backup we need (Matt 18:19-20). The Holy Spirit, however, also has a very special source of help for us in our waging of spiritual warfare. We know from Scripture that the Lord employs angels in His Service and warfare. Angels bring messages, give protection, assist in battles and strengthen people. Hebrews 1:14 refer to the angelic host as "ministering spirits sent forth to minister for those who will inherit salvation". These angels will engage in battle against the dark powers of this cosmos. Even after Jesus' wilderness experience and victory of 40 days, Matthew 4:11 tells us that "the devil left Him [Jesus], and angels came and ministered to Him". Likewise Revelation 12:7 reveals, "And war broke out in heaven: Michael and his angels fought with the dragon; and the dragon and his angels fought". Michael and the dragon were in direct conflict with each other, but angels of both opposing camps were involved. The staggering truth in all of this is that angels are enlisted for engagement in spiritual warfare *in answer to our prayers!* When Daniel prayed and fasted for 21 days, there actually was a battle in the heavenlies for 21 days. Daniel's prayers were influential in this warfare (Daniel 10:1-14). Amazingly, when Peter was in prison, the church prayed and an angel was sent to release Peter from his bonds! (Acts 12:1-11). Our prayers actually do cause the Lord to send angels into earthly matters. Stunning! In our spiritual warfare, we really do have *praying friends with us, the Holy Spirit within us and angels around us.*

Spiritual weapons:
10 The Assurance of our Final Victory

Great opportunity; great opposition; great overcoming – this is the normal Christian life for all, in the ongoing and inevitable spiritual warfare today.

Consider two men who underwent severe pain and suffering in the midst of spiritual warfare; note their lives of obedient service and faithfulness.

A. Suffering Job.

<u>**Job 1 – 2**</u>

Many of us, if we are honest with ourselves, accept the reality of spiritual warfare but fail fully to realise the seriousness of it today. We may tend to think of it as being personal temptation by the powers of darkness, intended to push us into sinful realms of thought, word and deed. That is certainly part of it, but by no means the whole of it. It is the global work of Satan and his armies to wreck and destroy the kingdom God will bring in through the work of Christ and the Spirit. Jesus summarised it by saying in John 10:10, "The thief comes only to steal and kill and destroy". The OT account of Job gives us remarkable insight into a behind-the-scenes case of intense spiritual warfare, in which Satan repeatedly assaults God's faithful and righteous servant Job, who 'feared God and shunned evil'. Satan is invited by God to test Job to the limit and Satan tries to prove that Job actually does not love God! (Job1:1-10) Satan then issues the crucial challenge to God, namely that if God were to threaten Job with multiple losses, then Job would curse God. It is at this point in 1:12 that God invites Satan to the effect that all Job's possessions are now under Satan's control, except that the Lord forbids Satan from touching Job's body. Satan leaves the Lord's presence and proceeds to strip away Job's possessions and children (Job 1:13ff). Systematic losses then follow up to 1:19.

Job responds in the expression of grief *and* worship (1:20-22). On another day, Satan comes again to join the sons of God in presenting himself before the Lord. Job 2:2-4 virtually repeats the text of Job 1:7-8, though Job 2 adds to verse 3 the phrase "He still holds fast his integrity, although you incited me (God) against him (Job) to destroy him (Job) without reason". Satan answers the Lord in 2:4 and insists, however, that a man will give simply anything for his life's preservation and that all the Lord has to do is to touch

Job's body (2:5) and Job will respond by cursing the Lord. The Lord then sets the limit by saying to Satan, "Behold, he is in your hand; only spare his life" (2:6). Satan then hits Job with multiple sores; Job's wife tells her husband to curse God, but Job perseveres in his pain. In Job 2:11ff, Job's three friends Eliphaz, Bildad and Zophar seek to offer comfort to their suffering friend, express grief and sit in silence with him for seven days (Job 2:12-13). Then Job curses his birth in 3:1.

So, Satan's root desire was to acquire from God permission to 'steal, kill and destroy', so that he (Satan) might see how painful misery would twist Job and turn him against the God he claimed to love! The staggering outcome, however, was that Job responded to all his pain *with worship* (Job 1:21). Because Job is righteous, he refuses to curse God. He does become frustrated with his friends who claim Job suffers because of some sins he has been guilty of. Job wants a divine explanation, but in Job 38-41, God appears and speaks 'out of the storm', revealing His power, magnificence and total knowledge! Job had realised that it was pointless to try to fully understand God and he realised that he had no right to demand anything of the Lord God.

So, what are we to learn from our reflections on the deep pain of Job? What are the lessons for our own involvement in Spiritual Warfare? In a nutshell, Satan's twin goal in spiritual warfare is to keep the unbelieving world in a state of spiritual ignorance, blindness and darkness, while at the same time to turn the believing people of God against God in their thinking, feeling and acting in their daily living. It is basically what Satan did in the Garden of Eden and in his testing of Jesus in the wilderness. In short, he will do what Jesus said he always did in John 10:10 ie. He will 'steal, kill and destroy'. He will tempt, reward and exploit. He will employ accusation, manipulation, deception and downright lying to achieve his ends. On the contrary, our task and challenge in the midst of pain and suffering is *to worship God.* This will not come naturally or easily. C.S. Lewis knew personal pain and agony in his life and he wrote that God does not call us to 'be happy' or to 'snap out of it' or to 'develop a positive mindset' but rather 'to worship God'.

So, how actually do we worship God? We worship God, not only when we sing, pray and witness, but when we realise that the Lord God is massively greater than we are. Job and his friends tried to think God out, to understand His ways in our lives and somehow to expect that God actually owed them an account or reasoning for His activities. However, when God finally came onto the scene, Job was totally overwhelmed, driven to humility and repentance, and persuaded simply *to trust this mighty God.*

Job and Jesus, however, testify that Satan does not give up his assaults on God's people; he comes back again and again, departing for a season but returning with renewed and sometimes intensified venom (Luke 4:13). Read Hebrews 11-12 and see how demonic plots do not shock or surprise God. Rather does God actually *use* Satan to carry out divine purposes and to show how righteous believers in Christ are enabled to live by faith and patiently await their promised share in eternal glory. Abraham, Moses, David and Samuel are just a few examples of a whole host of those who testified to the strength and power of God in weak human lives. They looked to Jesus and were enabled to do incredible and impossible things by God, in God and for God. The amazing thing is that God allows us, nay rejoices, when we *worship* in the midst of pain and suffering, by asking Him for actual help to trust Him, by coming to Him with repentance to receive forgiveness, by expressing to Him our frustrations, feelings and fears when life looks bleak, dark, uncertain and costly, by singing, by praying even a sentence or two, by holding to Scripture and by testifying to others of His greatness. In short, we need to be continually equipped with the armour of God, not in response to spiritual assaults, but *before the* attacks arrive. Job, the Psalmist and New Testament disciples have repeatedly shown persevering faith because they have been put into situations that demand *that they trust God and the character of God in the warfare.*

B. The Apostle Paul

2 Corinthians 10:1 – 6

These verses introduce us to the themes of chapters **10-13**, such as Paul's supposed inconsistency of being bold when absent and timid when present; the basic misunderstanding of Paul's ministry in the Corinthians' minds; the subtle threat of Paul's imminent visit. Paul's main concern was to focus on the actual situation of the church (disobedience), as opposed to the way it really ought to be (discipline). If it doesn't improve, Paul will use *spiritual weapons* to improve it!

Paul is addressing the whole church at Corinth in 10:1. Paul has been charged with being bold and strong only in his letter-writing, but in a strange irony, Paul actually refuses to be highly commanding in this letter opening. Rather he appeals to them in a purposeful yet emotional way of pleading "by the meekness and gentleness of Christ". In this way, Paul shows that sometimes his letters are actually gentle and sometimes if he is charged with being timid in personal dealings, then he is simply following Jesus' own example! (Matt 11:29). Sometimes he could be very stern in letter *and* person. Of course Jesus could also be very stern in denunciation *and* vital actions. See the sense of Paul's service and commitment in 2 Cor 6:3-10. We are called to be generous in our estimates of others, slow to take offence, able to bear reproach, above mere self-interest. The Corinthians are confusing meekness with weakness. Paul thus uses irony to shame his Corinthian readers. These readers had basically embraced a triumphalistic understanding of greatness! They had failed to grasp what Christian values were actually all about! The only 'humility' they knew was false humility in order to impress and obtain! Paul wants them to *change* before he arrives! Paul prefers to be gentle and meek, rather then stern. He wants the Corinthians to exercise discipline against the 'some people', the intruders, who have caused trouble for Paul. Those people had been thinking that Paul lives *by the standards of this world.* The original could be translated "according to the flesh" ie. mired in egocentricity and thus pushing God out to the periphery or beyond. More probably they have been accusing Paul of being an ineffective leader, a timid, mediocre preacher with too little experience to earn respect and allegiance from the Corinthians. He has not been the spiritual leader that they themselves claim to be!

Two passages in particular show the quality of Paul's life and responses to the hostile persecution he suffered at the hands of his critics – 1 Cor 4:9, 11-13 and 2 Cor 6:3-10. By contrast, Paul's critics among the Corinthians were confusing meekness with weakness, gentleness with servility, and had simply failed to grasp the meaning and practice of true Christian humility. Paul did not do arrogant one-upmanship. Rather did he follow the teaching and modeling of Jesus. There was here a radical clash of two hugely different worldviews. The intruders/influencers of the Corinthians had shaped their view of true leadership, not by the example of Christ and His gospel, but by the values of this world and were therefore evaluating Paul by a perverted set of criteria and ending up with the false conclusion that Paul was actually a very poor Christian leader! Paul sought to correct their false view of his leadership credentials! All so ironic in reality! In our current culture of 2023, of course, we have been so conditioned into subjective thinking that we often fail to judge at all and fail to recognise or acknowledge false teaching when it stares us in the face. The victim in all this, both then and now, is biblical truth. Moreover, the gospel is primary and non-negotiable. It is easy to follow the 'Christianised' version of our cultures and assume that that is the gospel! Very subtle demonic deception is surely in this. This is why Paul calls this belief system of the intruders 'another gospel' that true Christians need to avoid like the plague.

From **2 Cor 10:3-4a,** Paul starts to speak of the weapons that he uses, which are not 'of this world'. For Paul, 'eschatology' was at the same time both futuristic (not yet) and realised (now). The Corinthians leaned towards 'over-realised eschatology' by which they saw the future blessings of sinners, but had failed to be aware that until Christ's return, they were called to lives of self-denial and suffering. They stressed spiritual power, freedom and triumph. They were so spiritual that the things of this body and this life were of little interest to them. They measured spirituality according to rhetoric, wealth gained in preaching and the popularity of the preacher. Disastrous, because these are worldly weapons! 2 Cor 10:5 reveals Paul's contrary claim that the weapons he uses 'have divine power to demolish strongholds'. In other words, Paul's weapons are powerful because they are spiritual and are linked to God. Paul's weapons have the power to destroy human, sinful thinking ie. they demolish 'every pretension that sets itself up against the knowledge of God'. By cynicism, pride and independence, we have tried to live independently of God, because of which sin we have been given over to our depraved minds (Rom. 1:28-32). The only knowledge of God people need is the 'foolish' message of the crucified and risen Christ. We have been created by God to be dependent on Him but we rebelled against that divine wisdom. The root problem of sin is human pride. 2 Cor. 10:5 insists that these divine weapons have enough power to 'take captive every thought to make it obedient to Christ'. Indeed Christ brings these captured thoughts under a completely new authority and allegiance. What Paul is actually saying is that a conflict of minds is going on between spiritual enemies, that his weapons are getting results and that his weapons are producing transformed lives from place to place (2 Cor. 10:13-15a).

So what actually **are** Paul's powerful spiritual weapons that transform?

Most of these spiritual weapons can be deduced from 2 Cor 10-13, but we return briefly also to Paul's list already studied in Eph 6:13-18, namely the truth of the gospel; righteousness; prepared and ready from being rooted in a real grasp of the gospel of peace; faith; salvation; the Word of God; watchful prayer. The gospel of Christ is not rooted in worldly success, materialism, health, prosperity. Rather does it involve suffering, persecution, defeat, faithfulness and death. Believers should be bearing the fruit of God-centred worship, genuine repentance and faith, righteousness and humility. *Our responsibility in witness* is to pray for people, to proclaim and explain the gospel, live out the gospel of peace, walk a righteous life by faith. Listeners will eventually see our ultimate allegiance and our hugely different worldview. The outcome will be that the power of truth, the conviction by the Holy Spirit and the glory of Christ will work together to smash objections, reasons and arguments, until finally the seeker's mind and heart will be taken captive and obedient to Christ. This is how lives are changed by God. Only the use of divine, spiritual weapons can produce such stunning and lasting life transformation! In 2 Cor 10:6 the apostle says that he will be ready to punish acts of disobedience by these intruders, once the church has perfected its own obedience to completion by imposing discipline. Paul's great wish is that the church will take positive steps of its own accord. Once the church moves forward as one, in exercising discipline, then Paul will be willing to add any further strict discipline of his own.

2 Corinthians 12:1-10

See Carson pp. 161-185.

The deep pain and sufferings of Paul in his life and ministry are treated in several sections of 2 Corinthians, especially Chapters 1, 4, 6 and 11. In 11:30, the apostle declares, "if I must boast, I will boast of the things that show my weakness". This leads us into a very relevant and significant report of his stunning vision and his assessment of it. Likely was it that false apostles were claiming superiority in rhetoric, wealth, leadership, but also spirituality! Claims to visions and revelations would have been well received and would have enhanced their 'authority'. Paul is thus reluctantly ready to speak out his vision. Indeed he does actually concede here that the person who received this particular vision is Paul himself and it must have happened during AD 35-45, a time when we know almost nothing of Paul's life.

Paul had been caught up into the 'Paradise' of God's presence and thus the ultimate goal of every child of God. Paul genuinely doesn't know if he experienced this vision in a bodily state or spiritual state. (2 Cor. 12:2,3) It was inexpressible ie. unable to express or explain it. Paul could not give an account of it once he had returned to normality. The vision was purely for Paul's benefit, not the church's, so as to lift his spirits, so he could persevere in suffering to the end. In 2 Cor. 12:5-6a, Paul prefers to ponder and reflect on his present suffering and weakness, rather than on the glory that will be his later. The apostle did not want people to think *too* highly of him (12:6b). He didn't want anyone to assess him on the basis of his unprovable visions. Let folk measure him by his *behaviour*. Paul always wanted people to focus on Christ and His gospel, not on Paul himself as the preacher and messenger.

We now move into the vital section of **2 Cor 12:7-10**, regarding its importance for our own engagement in spiritual warfare today. Paul is ready to reveal the close link for believers between huge spiritual privileges and huge suffering. Many theories exist about the actual identity of the thorn in Paul's flesh, which came to him *after* his remarkable revelations and as a result of those great revelations. Paul had endured much pain as listed in 2 Corinthians, (1:8, 11:23) so the actual 'thorn' must presumably have been something even more serious than many pains. The apostle viewed the thorn as simultaneously the work of Satan *and* the work of God. This thorn was 'an angel ie. messenger of Satan', sent by Satan to damage him. Satan has power to tempt and seduce us morally, but also to cause us physical harm (Job 2:1-10; 1 Cor 5:5; 1 Tim. 1:20). Surely God normally wants to defeat Satan. This is a complex issue because Paul asserts this thorn came ultimately from God. He writes in the divine passive voice 'there was given me' ie. it was given to him *by God,* in order to keep Paul from becoming proud or arrogant. Only God would have had this positive goal to keep the apostle humble. We must beware of blaming Satan or God for specific events or works in our lives. Such a practice can cause us easily to speculate and misinterpret such events or works. For example, Jesus' cruel death is blamed on evil and manipulative people (Lk 22:53; Acts 2:23, 4:27). Yet, at the same time, Acts 4:28 says these happenings took place by what God's 'power and will had decided beforehand should happen'. In short, it was God's plan from the start, yet evil people were responsible for executing it! Similarly 'death' is biblically a victory but at the same time an enemy! We must maintain a balance in Scripture. 'Death' is not basically good, for it speaks of sin, curse and corruption, but God's grace is such that death opens the door to hope. Likewise, disease, accidents, persecution are not good and all these are indeed rooted in Satan, yet these things are not outside of God's sovereignty (Rom. 8:28).

The best translation of 2 Cor. 12:7 is "To keep me from becoming conceited because of these surpassingly great revelations, there was given me a thorn in my flesh, a messenger of Satan, to torment me". There was nothing basically good about this thorn, but it was given by God for beneficial purposes! A parallel OT situation would be the case of Joseph being sold by his brothers into slavery, yet years later Joseph could declare to his brothers, "You intended to harm me, but God intended it for good to accomplish what is now being done, the saving of many lives" (Gen. 50:20). God planned the thorn for Paul because of the massive revelations in order to stop the apostle becoming conceited. How dangerous is self-exaltation. Paul really has learnt his lesson, as he makes clear in 2 Cor. 12:8-9a.

However, it clearly *was* really tough for Paul to bear this thorn, as evidenced by his three lengthy periods of prayer to Jesus to be freed from this pain. Instead of taking away the thorn, God promises. "My grace is sufficient for you, for my power is made perfect in weakness (2 Cor. 12:9a). Paul had wanted relief and respite from the thorn by having it removed, but God added grace so Paul could bear the thorn *in his weakness.* Jesus said in Matt 5:3 that the kingdom of heaven goes to the poor and weak in spirit. We need to remember that Paul's thorn is not followed by healing; instead, grace is given to him to equip him to deal with the weakness *that is not taken away*. Grace is a *continuing* mechanism. Christians are 'more than conquerors' in the contexts of hardship, famine, sword and trouble. God loves us *in the midst* of such struggle (Rom. 8:31-39).

In **2 Cor. 12:9b-10,** Paul finally recongnises the wisdom of God's response to Paul's appeals for delivery from his struggles. The apostle declares, "Therefore I will boast all the more gladly about my weaknesses, so that Christ's power may rest on me. That is why, for Christ's sake, I delight in weaknesses, in insults, in hardships, in persecutions, in difficulties. For when I am weak, then I am strong". Paul is ready to boast of his weaknesses if it means the power of Christ will remain on him. Christ longs to achieve His greatest results by doing works of power, using powerless instruments. The false apostles and teachers in Corinth and elsewhere simply would not get it! Paul's boasting of his weaknesses would be virtually meaningless to them. Only those who serve and suffer 'for Christ's sake' (2 Cor 12:10) can go forward in humble trust of, and discipleship towards, this Suffering Servant, the Lord Jesus Christ Himself.

It is to the example of Christ that we now finally turn, for He established a pattern for Christian life and ministry, rooted in the simply appalling death to which He voluntarily submitted. The Roman cross was a symbol of shame, defeat, judgment and humiliating disgrace. Yet, incredibly, this shocking death, in the context of spiritual warfare, was exactly the means by which Jesus triumphed over all His enemies. It was, and still remains, the ultimate demonstration of God's strength in Jesus' weakness, as He surrendered to death but was raised to eternal rule!

CONCLUSION: The Centrality of Christ in Spiritual Warfare

JESUS THE SUPREME OVERCOMER.

A. Jesus overcomes – by his authority over the 'powers'.

Matthew's teaching on the nature and challenges of Christian discipleship fills much of the major section, namely Chapters 5-7. The people concluded in Matt 7:28-29 that "when Jesus finished these sayings, the crowds were astonished at his teaching, for He was teaching them as one who had authority, and not as their scribes". Jesus' *teaching* with authority is absolutely crucial, but then so are His *acts* of authority. Matthew underlines this fact in 4:23-25, but then fills Chapters 8-9 with evidence of Jesus' miraculous activity throughout the Galilee region (9:8,32-34). So, Jesus came not only to teach but to demonstrate His authority revealed in His works of power. He then develops in Matt 10 his related key themes of mission and discipleship. These accounts all lead towards Matthew's stunning claim that Jesus really is the true Messiah of God. Ultimately therefore, Jesus as Messiah, does have the divine authority to call us to *discipleship* and such discipleship is at times painful and costly.

Matthew records five specific exorcisms: **8**:28-34; **9**:32-33; **12**:22; **15**:21-28; **17**:14-20. In the first, he presents an actual exorcism carried out by Jesus. Its sheer shortness, without preamble, magic or formulas, highlights just how powerfully Jesus deals with the two possessed Gadarene demoniacs: in verse 32, Jesus issues the simple but devastating command, "Go!" The demons have no choice whatsoever. Immediately they rush into the herd of pigs and the pigs race into the sea where they are drowned. The Son of God had total authority over them! Two spiritual authorities are in direct confrontation, clash and collision. It is the fate of the pigs and demons, not the men, that is the central focus. The location of this miracle was the eastern shore of Galilee, a largely non-Jewish area where the two violent men inhabited an 'unclean' tomb and the demons swept into 'unclean' animals – pigs. The demons had recognised the identity of Jesus as 'Son of God'. Interestingly, and very significantly, we are made aware in 8:29 that not only did the demons recognise a supernatural Jesus, but they knew that their allotted time to harass humans was limited – "before the proper time" – and that Jesus' presence there indicated the beginning of the end for the demons' evil work! The incarnate Jesus had opened an eschatological shift in God's programme to start dealing with evil.

The disciples were slow on the uptake to grasp this truth. Are we any better in our mindset re spiritual warfare and overcoming? Demons as supernatural beings could not be destroyed by drowning, but the key truth is that the demons were subject to Jesus' complete control and authority. The Christ had His Hand on the entire situation from start to end! Pigs do not naturally act *as a herd*, and they don't stampede over a cliff! The crowd was very disturbed and sought to persuade Jesus to get out of their territory. They were simply terrified by this dramatic expression of Jesus' sheer authority.

A brief look at another of Jesus' exorcisms in **Matt 17:14-20** will enhance our understanding of His supernatural authority over the demonic world. An anxious father pleads for help from Jesus because the Messiah's disciples had failed to deal with the son's repeated and distressing fits. Jesus expresses His frustration. The text indicated an emotional exclamation from Jesus' lips, targeted at the faithless generation he faces. He addresses *all disciples* and challenges them over their failure to engage in spiritual warfare. What is Matthew saying to us all on this matter? Matt 17:19 indicates that the disciples are somewhat mystified regarding their failure to drive out the demon.

The text seems to be stressing that only Jesus has power to heal and cast out demons; disciples must draw on this authority *by faith*. The strongest lesson to be learnt is for the disciples themselves. Compared with the other Gospel accounts, Matthew has reduced the length of the narrative and focused instead on the teaching element and lessons to be grasped. When Jesus acts against a demon, it is either because He takes the initiative to deal with defiant demons or in response to a parental plea. Possessed folk themselves don't have the power or initiative to go directly to Jesus for help. We must not make a direct automatic equating of epilepsy with demon-possession. Jesus' frustration is aimed at the *whole generation,* not merely the disciples following their mountaintop experience. Jesus eventually tells the disciples to bring the boy to Him and the Lord rebukes and expels the demon instantly. The disciples should have prayed to God for His power to be manifested. Jesus is not asking disciples to have a certain quantity of faith, but rather to have even a tiny mustard seed of faith that can draw on the unlimited power of God. The disciples had failed to exercise any faith at all! That is a lesson for all Jesus' disciples!

B. Jesus overcomes – by his power over sickness, nature and death

At the start of Matthew 8 we notice the deliberate choice of three healing incidents – a leper who was inevitably an outcast from regular society; a Gentile centurion who was probably Matthew's servant; a woman who was Peter's mother-in-law. Each of these three healings involved social, as well as physical, aspects. The leper finds social normality through his healing while the Gentile and the woman find not only healing, but also an acceptance with Jesus, the Israelite Messiah of God. The acceptance of Gentiles into the Kingdom of God is key here.

Lepers were counted as ritually unclean and thus isolated. Once healed however, and the appropriate offerings made as required by the priest, a return to normality was possible. Leprosy was basically impossible to cure in any physical sense and the ancient world considered such healing on a par with being raised from the dead. Here then is the significance of this healing, namely that it underlined the divine authority and power that Jesus really did possess. This was a much-feared illness right across society and the fact that Jesus actually *touched* the leper, underlined to onlookers the sheer power, courage and deep compassion of this Messiah from God. The leper was instantly healed by Jesus, but even the leper's addressing of Jesus as 'Lord' and his wondering whether Jesus would actually be *willing* to heal someone like him, strongly suggest that the leper knew something utterly extraordinary was likely to happen in their midst because a staggering divine authority and power was about to be exercised and seen! The priest would clearly *see* this demonstration of divine power and there is a sense in which such a healing does ultimately constitute a *witness* not only as required by the priest, but as pointing to the global power of the gospel. That gospel is the power available to us now in the challenge of Spiritual Warfare.

In **Matt 8:5-13** a non-Jew approaches Jesus for divine help. This Gentile centurion had a very sick servant but initially Jesus, the Jewish Messiah, seems somewhat reluctant to offer healing. Until, that is, Jesus is stunned at this remarkable expression of Gentile faith in a Jewish healer. The centurion has the faith to believe that *a word from Jesus,* albeit at a distance and without Jesus' presence or touch, will be sufficient to secure healing. Jesus' authority alone will be enough, just as the centurion himself exercises words of authority in his own military work! Jesus is impressed, to put it mildly. Jesus issues a thinly-veiled rebuke to Jews that this Gentile's faith far surpasses that of many of the Jews! Many Gentiles will take places in the Banquet. Jesus healed by a word of authority without entering the

Gentile home in person. It is significant that the centurion twice addresses Jesus as 'Lord'. Clearly he expected something big to happen and he was not disappointed with the result. Jesus had authority and power over all forms of opposition. In verse 9 the key revelation is the affirmation of Jesus' unquestioned spiritual authority. Faith is rooted here and elsewhere in the Gospels as the practical conviction that Jesus really does have the authority to heal. That is beyond all doubt. This great truth of course has massive implications also for His authority to equip His disciples with power for spiritual battle. In verses 11-12, Matthew extends the practical faith of healing contexts to the issue of the faith that brings Gentiles, as well as repentant Jews, into true membership of the kingdom of heaven. Matthew is unafraid to claim, especially in later chapters, that the true people of God will not be based on racial ancestry, but rather on the basis of faith in Jesus. The shock is that the 'sons of the kingdom' will be excluded from the banquet and will be in the very place they had reserved for the ungodly. The faith of this centurion and the authoritative words of Jesus will combine to establish the final glorious kingdom of God. That is the sheer authority and power by which Jesus will defeat all that works against such a kingdom!

Matthew 8:14-17 presents the case of Jesus' healing of Peter's mother-in-law. Simon Peter apparently had a home and family in Capernaum and on this occasion, Jesus was in that house and dealt with the sick mother-in-law of Peter. Jesus touched the woman and it seems the case that she was immediately healed. She immediately served the needs of her household, without a moment of recovery or rest! Verses 16-17 describe a number of healings "in the evening" and we are simply told that Jesus drove out demons "with a command". The focus yet again is on the absolute authority of this Jesus. The reference to the Suffering Servant section of Isaiah 52:13 – 53:12 quotes, "He Himself took up our weaknesses and carried our illnesses". Traditional interpretation refers to Jesus' role as bearing the sins of His people. Matthew does however focus on the Hebrew terms of 'illnesses' and 'pains' that point to Jesus as a holistic healer, not just His suffering and death.

A different case of Jesus' supernatural authority and power is that recorded by Matthew in the so-called 'Stilling of the Storm' in 8:23-27. A similar miracle in 14:33 persuaded the disciples that Jesus was indeed the Son of God who had control over the natural world. God had clearly come to this world in "Christ". We know from the OT that God was recognised as exerting control over the wind and the waves (Job 38:8-11; Psalms 65:5-8;

89:8-9; 107:23-30). Matthew treats this event on three levels, namely the sheer magnificence of the miracle itself, but also the extent of Jesus' control of the whole situation, although also the sad truth that the disciples had failed to exercise trust. Remarkable it was that the nautically competent Galilean fishermen were turning for help to a man with far less knowledge of sailing. They knew they needed something truly extraordinary to happen, by someone who Himself owned extraordinary powers of intervention. In the story of Jonah, the crew of the sinking ship had to wake Jonah in the middle of the storm, so that Jonah could pray to his God for the needed help for boat and crew. By contrast, Jesus dealt first of all with the issue of human fear and divine faith, before rising to deal with the challenge *by His own authority* rather than by praying for God's help. Such was Jesus' complete control of the whole situation. After all, Jesus had created that very same sea! The disciples had failed to grasp God's care for them in every situation they would face in their following of this Christ.

As Matthew moves his records of Jesus' authority and power from Chapter 8 into Chapter 9, subtle changes begin to appear in the reporting of audience responses to Jesus. Jews had been attracted by Jesus' miracles, but in the Gentile Decapolis area, people wanted rid of Him. Even among His own people, some were disturbed by His exorcist activity. It was not that His power was doubted by such critics, but rather that they questioned the *source* of that power. *Just who actually was this Christ, and what was the mission* of this travelling 'holy man'?

Matt 9:1-8 presents his readers with what seems like a physical ailment of paralysis, presented to Jesus in Capernaum. Jesus does indeed deal with this plea and the man immediately regains full health. *However,* Matthew reveals a strange 'twist-in-the-tail', in the form of a subplot, in which Jesus suddenly but significantly, displays His authority to *forgive sins,* to the sheer horror of the scribes who smell here a blasphemy! Jesus is asserting his spiritual authority to deal not only with sickness but also with sinfulness itself. The start of real tension, yet not so strange really in a world with some fluidity between spiritual and physical ills and in any case, Matthew had already commented in 1:21 on Jesus' mission as including the reality that "He will save his people from their sins". Matthew is not claiming that the paralysis was caused by the sin that Jesus forgives. That Jesus is forgiving sins by His own authority is surely what is deeply disturbing for the scribes, because there has been no mention of a formal atonement. Surely God alone could forgive sin!! Matthew has raised a massive issue here, regarding the authority and power of this Jewish Messiah. Verse 4 also recongnises that

Jesus has supernatural insight into human thoughts. He knows what goes on in our minds and internal beings. Matthew is moving his Gospel into deeper and deeper realms that expose the very deepest need of humans to identify, acknowledge and seek divine help to forgive that sinfulness that is rooted in all of our lives – in thoughts, words and deeds.

In verses 5-6 some would think that forgiving sins would be harder than healing paralysis, since only God can forgive sins. However, Jesus is asking which option is easier to *say, not do.* Anyone can claim to forgive sins since it cannot be verified or falsified, whereas healing a paralytic can be proved true or false by what is visible! Since Jesus healed this paralytic, this constitutes evidence that He also has authority to forgive sins. In verse 6, Jesus addresses the scribes but this leads into a main clause that is a command to the paralytic. As the man is told to get up and go home, this constitutes proof of the claim made by Jesus. Both parts of the sentence are true and valid. Jesus has divine authority *both to heal the paralytic and to forgive his sins*! Jesus, Son of Man, and God actually share the authority to forgive sins. Jesus on earth is authorised to issue God's forgiveness.

Matthew presses on in 9:7-8 with his report of this truly remarkable incident. The healing just witnessed triggers *fear*! Why fear? Probably not related to the healing *per se* but rather to the whole truth that this healer, the Christ, had authority to forgive sins. This authority has been given to just one person, the Lord Jesus Christ. In short, Matthew places his emphasis on *Jesus' unique authority to forgive sins.* Matthew is leading us in a very particular and extremely important direction, namely sin!

The section **9:9-17** sees Matthew revealing Jesus as someone who looks for true disciples, not mainly among the comfortable and respectable, but rather among those shunned by society. He seeks followers among those who see their spiritual need. After all, He came to "save His people from their sins" (1:21). Jesus is looking for those who will come to Him in need, casting themselves upon Him and longing to live a new life by the Spirit. Jesus willingness to share a meal with those despised tax collectors and probably women as well, clearly aroused the indignation of the scribes and Pharisees, made even stronger by its location in the "unclean" house of a tax collector! The use of the term 'your teacher' in 9:11 by the Pharisees was probably sarcastic. In verses 12-13, Jesus is getting across the point that in the true kingdom of heaven, mercy is deemed higher than sacrifice. Jesus called sinners like Matthew so they could turn from sin and find true righteousness.

One very significant point in 9:15 regarding the joyful celebration at a wedding feast is the sudden and jarring mention of a future time when the 'Bridegroom [Jesus] is taken away from them, and then they will fast.' This is the first hint of Jesus' violent exit from this world, a theme that is expanded from 16:21 onwards. The wineskins parable in 9:16-17 hints at the need for the newness of the kingdom in Christ to be constantly lived out, while the 'oldness' of former ways of sacrifices, ritual and religious tradition needs to be left behind.

In his section **9:18-34,** Matthew includes more cases of spiritual and physical deliverance which submit to the authority and power of Jesus. Matthew focuses not so much on great detail, but rather on audience responses, on joyful celebration of victory and on the high demands of Christian discipleship. People in bondage are set free from death, demons, disease and danger. Spiritual warfare must not be allowed to rob us of joy and rejoicing in the Lord's victory. Matt 9:18-26 does indeed describe Jesus' raising of the official's dead daughter. The healing of the woman with the lengthy period of hemorrhage significantly blends the themes of impurity, healing, faith and salvation. Matthew gradually deepens our grasp of just what actually was happening in these remarkable events. We must note also the holding of the dead girl's hand by Jesus and the touching of Jesus' cloak by the sick woman. A stunning example of Jesus' smashing His way through centuries of Jewish religious taboo and tradition! Incredible indeed were these two events! Jesus' own resurrection has overcome the finality of death itself, but such a realisation would not have been obvious to the spectators. Sadly Matthew later records in 11:20-24 that even in the areas where these miracles had been witnessed, there was a serious and severe dearth of the needed human response of repentance. How hard were the hearts and stubborn the wills!

Jesus in 9:28-29 on the occasion of the healing of two blind men actually *insists* on a declaration from these men that they really do believe that Jesus has the authority and power to heal them. Remarkable that they had this level of trust in a man they had never in their lives actually *seen* until He healed them! Jesus uses a strong word meaning "warned fiercely" only here in his entire Gospel to underline the need for the complete silence of these two healed men! Why? Perhaps it was because these men were the first to call Jesus "Son of David" ie Messiah. Perhaps Jesus was safe-guarding Himself against the growing mix of responses to Jesus' life and ministry. Thus, in the healing of the man unable to speak, which follows in 9:32-34, Jesus drives out a demon before healing the mute man. The crowd massively marveled at Jesus' power and authority in both healing and exorcism. However, the other extreme of response was displayed by the Pharisees' severe and negative opposition to the exorcism. The Pharisees' suggestion that the 'prince of demons' lies behind Jesus' power, is simply horrendous and highly offensive. They flatly rejected His claim to divine authority, and thus brought His clash with the Pharisees onto hostility of a new level. The parting of the ways was now inevitable. Jesus was in deep trouble and formed a prelude to Jesus' open statement in 9:35-38 that His mission in life was to win folk, by His shared gospel, authority and power.

C. Jesus overcomes evil, sin and death – by His death on the cross and by His resurrection from the grave

Matthew moves forward in his Gospel from Chapter 10 by Jesus' sending out of the disciples. These followers of Jesus were the recipients of Jesus' ministry, but now they are to become its agents, sharing in the proclamation and works of the gospel, rooted in the authority of the Messiah Himself. Mission remains central, but alongside that is the issue of the hostile response to Jesus and to His disciples. They will be persecuted.

We move now from the focus on *the authority and power of Jesus* towards *the sharing* of that authority and power with his disciples throughout the ages for the continuation of Christian mission and ministry to all nations. The key to our understanding of how this 'transfer' from Christ into our own lives takes place in reality and requires three stages of thought.

i) How did the dying and rising of Jesus achieve *victory*?

Even by a brief reading of **Mark**'s Gospel, the overriding impression we get is that the entire gospel is moving, step-by-step, towards the death and resurrection of Jesus. In 1:1-8 the Trinity of Father, Son and Holy Spirit is present and within a few verses there is a call to repent and believe in the gospel. Those who heard Jesus recognised His authority, and the demons recognised the Sonship of Jesus. This Christ repeatedly heals and drives out demons. Jesus is not afraid to confess that He came, not to call the righteous, but sinners. However, in 2:20 Jesus points to Himself as the "bridegroom who will be taken away," and Mark 3 reports early human plans to destroy Jesus, while the scribes thought Jesus Himself was possessed! Yet, the Gerasene demoniac in 5:1-20 recognised Jesus as "Son of the Most High God". Crowds marveled at the deliverances, but some were terrified and urged Jesus to depart. Jesus in 6:7-13 gives His disciples the authority to set free those in bondage. Jesus names specific sins in 7:20-23, but some hearts are hardened and Jesus collides repeatedly with the Scribes, Pharisees and teachers of the Law.

Even Jesus' own disciples fail to understand the authority and power of Jesus, as seen in the feeding of the 4000 and 5000. Yet, Jesus insists that He must suffer, be rejected, be killed and then be raised. Peter doesn't get it and Jesus sees this as Satan's voice in 8:31-38! Repeatedly, Jesus warns His disciples not to spread news of Jesus' ministry. His coming death and resurrection is predicted by Jesus again in 9:30-32, and then again in 10:32-34. Jesus will give His life "as a ransom for many". Disciples will be hated and persecuted but "those who endure to the end will be saved", says 13:13. Days of tribulation will come, but the End is not yet here. A woman anoints Jesus with oil in anticipation of His burial. Further predictions of His death and resurrection are recorded in 14:22-25. Jesus is finally deserted and Pilate hands Jesus over to be crucified in 15:6-15.

We then read of the rapid succession of the final events of Jesus' life, death and rising, spelled out in Mark's closing two chapters:

Crucifixion in 15:21-32 describes Simon of Cyrene carrying the cross for the massively weakened Jesus, who refuses the offer of wine and myrrh. Jesus continued to be insulted and mocked in calls from the by-passers. The Lord and Saviour was suffering in overwhelming physical pain, was facing the social disgrace of a criminal's dying in the presence of family and onlookers, but most of all, was experiencing the appalling spiritual darkness of actual separation from His Father, as He bore the appalling weight of the totality of the sin of all who would turn to Him.

Death for Jesus is recorded in 15:33-41, under the three hours of physical darkness in which Jesus cried, "My God, my God, why have you forsaken me?" Jesus dies and the Temple curtain is split into two.

Jesus' *Burial* is noted in 15:42-47 as Joseph of Arimathea asks Pilate for Jesus' body and lays it in a tomb with a stone rolled across the entrance.

Then the *Resurrection* of Jesus in 16:1-8 explains that the women and Salome took spices to anoint Jesus, but they discovered the stone already rolled back, with a young man seated inside who urges the women not to be alarmed, for Jesus had been raised. Their task was to tell His disciples and Peter. The section Mark 16:9-20 is the disputed closing record of the command of Jesus to preach the gospel.

Mark's great goal in writing of Jesus' life and ministry is highlighted very decisively in 1:14-15. The crucial two verbs are "repent" and "believe/trust in the gospel" which denote conversion into discipleship. In other words, 'be converted'. It basically means an intellectual acceptance of the gospel's truth but also a response and commitment to that gospel, but as the time of Jesus' death approaches, there would be many who struggled to grasp any concept of a powerful, life-changing gospel! After all, Jesus was locked into the hands of all his enemies. He Himself showed no signs of resistance whatsoever, even if He was capable. He was utterly mocked and humiliated from all quarters and His status as Son of God and King of the Jews must have seemed utterly ludicrous in light of His battered body and blooded brow. What incredible irony. See Ps. 22 for clear parallels of language. How on earth could Jesus even be considered as capable of saving *anyone,* let alone thinking that somehow He was achieving a success or a *victory*? The very idea was totally bizzare! The Jews were incensed that Jesus claimed any relationship with God, while the Romans charged Him with political treason because for anyone to claim kingship within the Roman Empire was automatically guilty of treason. Yet here was an innocent man heading for a brutal death amid disgrace, mockery, insult and humiliation. No wonder the Roman orator Cicero, just a mere few decades before Jesus' time, felt compelled to write of crucifixion, "It is a most cruel and disgusting punishment.... Let the very word 'cross' be far removed from not only the bodies of Roman citizens, but even from their thoughts, their eyes and their ears".

The unnatural and eerie darkness that fell upon the scene for around three hours signaled the absolute uniqueness of this crucifixion. Daytime blackness displayed the displeasure and judgment of God, not on Jesus Christ, but on human sin. A pagan centurion cried out, "Truly this was the Son of God"! Around the same time, the ripping of the Temple curtain from top to bottom signified the opening of access for willing humanity into the very holiness and presence of God Himself. Jesus' final shout "My God, My God, why have you forsaken me?" must have sounded like a deep cry of despair rather than a shout of success, triumph or *victory*! But why such a horrendous death for a Messiah? Mark gives us hints such as "a ransom for many" (Mk 10:45) and "the blood of the covenant" (Mk 14:24). Gospel core indeed! Jesus' final shout took every ounce of strength He could possibly muster, out of His completely weakened and drained body. Yet here again lies the sheer irony of His dying – His weakness made certain the release of a power that this earth had never seen – the power of the gospel of God. How stunning though that this happened at the point of Jesus' own sense of His complete abandonment by His Father. Mark however at this point is keen that we *feel the depth of Jesus' pain* rather than trying to explain it all.

Highly significant through all these stages of Jesus' suffering was the presence of a faithful group of His disciples. They were all women, such as Mary Magdalene, Mary the mother of James the younger and of Joses, and Salome. As RT France writes in his commentary on Mark (2002:661) "They saw him die, they saw him buried and they saw that same tomb empty". Jesus had a wide following among women. When all the male disciples had fled, the women were still present and faithful to Jesus. This is a new stage of discipleship and it was to these women that the news and message of Jesus' victorious resurrection was first entrusted. The gospels combine to confirm that following His crucifixion, death, and burial, Jesus rose from the grave, leaving the tomb empty and defying and defeating death itself. He overcame our last enemy, namely death itself, by His victorious resurrection. The huge stone across the tomb entrance had already been rolled away and the 'young man' must surely have been an angelic being who confirmed the truth and reality of Jesus having been raised from the dead. Mk 16:6-7 notes the stunning message from this angel that the women should tell the disciples *and Peter* that the bodily risen Jesus wants to meet and receive them in Galilee where it all began. God in Christ longs to redeem and forgive folk! We are left with a risen Christ and the Gospels underline very clearly and decisively that this resurrection is indeed a victory, but not only that. This victory *must be lived and worked out globally in Christian mission and discipleship, not to mention in our willingness to fight in spiritual warfare!!* This challenge to World Mission must have got through to the disciples in spite of the fears of the women! Fear is the currency Satan trades in and it holds us back from engagement in spiritual warfare. Hence our next section.

Jesus' victory over *Satan, Evil, Sin and Death* was, and is, absolutely complete! The Apostle Paul in 1 Corinthians 1:18 called the message of the Cross "the foolishness of God" – the sheer stupidity of God – "to those who are perishing, but to us who are being saved it is the power of God". This is indeed the massive theology that underlies the victory of God in Jesus' death, burial, resurrection, ascension and rule.

ii) How does this *victory* relate to/connect with our own Christian lives today, especially with regard to warfare?

a) On the <u>Cosmic Level</u> –

Let's summarise what John has concluded in his Book of Revelation 20:1- 15. Scholars differ on the issue of the Millennium or Thousand Year reign of Christ. Many believe that this started with the Resurrection of

Christ and will end with His Final Return. In other words, the Church Age. In this period, God limits Satan's power to deceive but it ends with a renewal and escalation of Satanic power against the Church and with God's final judgment of *all people*. Satan always employs his key weapon of *deception*. Rev 12:7-11 and 20:1-6 record visions that move from heaven to earth – Satan is ejected, but Christ and His people are *enthroned!* Satan's power is slowly but surely stripped away from Him. His anger rises in the short time left! The saints have come to life *by Christ's dying and rising, and this is the recurring and absolutely vital element in our understanding of our need to engage in spiritual warfare now.* There will indeed be human, global opposition to the global church in the closing days of this Church Age. Rev 20:10 – probably a repeat of 19:17-21 – confirms that it is Satan who has deceived the nations into attacking the godly. Beast, False Prophet and Satan will most likely be thrown into the lake of fire simultaneously, and along with all unbelievers, will face eternal, conscious punishment. (14:10-11). This is final judgment, taking place at the destruction and re-creation of the cosmos – the 'second death'. First death is physical and lasts till the destruction of the present cosmos. Unbelievers who die are held in 'death and Hades' until their final judgment into the 'lake'. Believers who die are kept by God in His Presence till Christ returns. 'Second death' cannot start till all have died physically and this cannot occur until the great white throne in 20:11-15. At that judgment after the Millennium, Death and Hades yield their dead for judgment and throwing into the 'lake'. Thus the battle and lake of 19:17-21 are the same events as 20:7-10 and the Millennium is therefore *before that battle ie. the Church Age.* The 'second death' lasts for ever and means eternal separation from God's Presence. 20:15 shows that God's holiness and justice absolutely compel Him to carry out judgment. *But our identification with Christ in His death and resurrection guarantee our eternal redemption. Christ our righteousness has freed us from judgment because he has already suffered our judgment in His body and in our place. 'Substitutionary Atonement'!*

After the dissolution of the cosmos, the new heaven and the new earth descend from God and the redeemed Church of Christ lives in the eternal presence of God. God's faithful saints will live in God's communion and community. Rev 1-3 had focused on the weak and much-failed churches of Asia Minor. By contrast, the churches of 21:1-8 are eternal and perfected. That is why believers here and now are urged to press on, to persevere, even in pain, in order to reach that perfected state. The new creation is recognisable but is renewed, and our new resurrection bodies will be identifiable. *New creation is linked to Christ's resurrection and ours.* Suffering will not be present in this new creation. A crucial verse is Rev 21:7 in which it is promised that in Christ, we will inherit what Christ inherits, but the ungodly will be excluded from God's Presence, including unbelievers, cowardly, idolaters, liars, persecutors of Christians, and professing believers who simply do not live out new lives. These will all enter the 'lake of fire', separated from God and in permanent spiritual pain – the 'second death'. Believers in glory will not float on clouds or stars, but will live in a renewed creation and in a raised and changed body, enjoying a *deeply intimate relationship with God.* No longer will they be in a shallow, unreal, pleasure-seeking world. This new world will be those who are '*overcomers*' – believers who persevere in hardship in order to inherit final glory! Yet again, we encounter this whole idea of the necessity of our *overcoming.* This vital theme now continues, not only on a cosmic level but in our own lives

b) On the Personal, Communal and Corporate Level –
Where better can we turn to in Scripture than to Colossians to get a grip, not only on the vertical importance of Jesus' death and resurrection, but also on its horizontal role in equipping us *to live out this new life of the Kingdom*?

By the death and resurrection of Jesus, as we come to Him in repentance and faith, we receive reconciliation, redemption and renewal, on the basis of Jesus' free gift of righteousness. That is, as it were, the vertical transaction; but we must then copy, match and live out that horizontal sequence of stages that Jesus experienced, for that is how we move forward in our Christian lives, by following the 'pattern' of Jesus' life and death, even though of course the Christ was without sin. Jesus died, was buried and was raised. We must hear and adopt this similar parallel that the Apostle Paul spelled out in Colossians 2-3. Thus, we were 'dead in our sins and in the uncircumcision of our sinful natures' (2:13); 'we were circumcised in the putting off of the sinful nature' (2:11); 'we were forgiven all our sins' (2:13); 'we died with Christ' (2:20); 'we were buried with Christ in baptism' (2:12); 'we were raised with Christ by faith' (2:12) and 'we are now alive with Christ' (2:13). Supremely of course, we now live in union *with Christ.* This means that our death with Christ has severed our links with our former existence, whilst our resurrection with Christ has brought us into a new level of existence. We are called to reveal Christ on earth in all we think, speak and do. This means putting to death the old life (3:5-9) and putting on the new life (3:10-14). Yes, the new power for the new life comes from God's Holy Spirit, but it is only possible because of our new position in Christ, having *died with Christ, been buried with Christ and been raised with Christ* ***already in this life***.

Our union with Christ transforms our minds, our hearts and our wills. We take part now in the resurrection life of Christ. Christ is continually empowering us for life and ministry and we need to depend continually on Him. This is especially the case when we are in the midst of the struggle, pain and opposition that come to us during Spiritual Warfare. That is the true, acid test of our faith, as Satan seeks to test the reality of our trust in the Lord. It will sometimes feel as if we are being punished for being an active, energetic Christian, but our calling is to endurance, perseverance and overcoming always.

iii) How does Jesus' *victory* equip us to be the 'overcomers' in the Spiritual Warfare that He requires of every true disciple of Christ?

Let's take a long look at John's vision in **Rev 12:11.** Single Bible Verses are generally somewhat risky, exegetically speaking, so let's consider initially the surrounding literary context of 12:11. The central section of Revelation – Chapters 12-14, located between the trumpets and bowls – includes a few digressions of which 12:7-12 is one, focussing on the past, heavenly viewpoint on what God is engineering in His cosmos. In 12:1, the woman is Jesus' mother, but there are also nudges in the direction of the tale of Eve and of God's promise (Rev 12:9,17) that the woman's seed would eventually crush the serpent (Gen 3:15). The 'woman' can also accommodate the idea of the people of God. In 12:2-3, John makes reference to the ancient serpent of 12:9, who pushed Adam and Eve to disobey God. For John, Christ is the one who will finally destroy the dragon and beast, as they manipulate even Roman emperors! For John, Satan rebels, along with his angelic workers of evil, in their combined attempt to smash Jesus' mission on the earth (12:4). Satan and his angels, however, catastrophically fail because of Jesus' death and resurrection. In Rev 12:5-6 John views the child as the Christ. Yes, Christ's servants also rule but only as they are united with Christ. John uses the theme of the desert to look back to the ancient Exodus, but applies it to us today by proclaiming a spiritual new exodus and delivery! The woman also 'bears' many other children who will be disciples of Jesus (12:17). This is the heart of all revelation and history. Jesus becomes King by His Resurrection and place on the throne. At the Cross, Satan was hurled down from heaven. Thus, C.S Keener concludes in his *Application Commentary* (2000:319) that "Christians are already living in the final era, regardless of that era's length". Satan has *already* been defeated. Thus, the arrival of God's kingdom and His saving work, coincide with Jesus' death, resurrection and final enthronement.

Rev 12:7-12 reveals a heavenly conflict that had already been won by Christ at the Cross of Calvary. Michael and his angels are at the heart of the heavenly victory won on earth by Christ. God controls this world via heavenly events and sets these events according to His activity on earth! Satan is constantly working on earth to disrupt the Kingdom of God. Satan's defeat in heaven, however, does not end the believers' physical pain here on earth. Herein lies a massive part of our overcoming Satan in Spiritual warfare, namely by faithfully witnessing to Christ's victory, even to death. Such testimony will speed up Christ's Second Coming. Never forget that the conquering Lion achieved such victory by taking the part of a slain Lamb! Satan will incessantly pursue us with deception and repression, and we will experience both unnerving suspense and agonizing hardship, even though the outcome is in fact guaranteed. God has set the time of judgment and fulfillment, on the completion of His great plan, and that is when the devil's merciless assault on the Kingdom simply has to run out! Yet, in all of this, God will keep us in the midst of unfair opposition, debilitating accusation and blasphemous slander from our great enemy. True, believing, righteous disciples of Jesus keep God's commandments, thereby holding the testimony of Jesus, and being prepared to die.

What then are the crucial applications of Jesus' victory that need to be manifested in our lives, as evidence that we are consistently 'overcomers' in Spiritual Warfare? Here are the marks of a genuine, practising disciple of Christ today –

a. Christian suffering simply cannot be separated from the preac boldly hing of the gospel of Christ. In secular, materialistic societies like the UK, supernatural evil raises its heads in many subtle and concealed ways. Christians are called not to make peace and agreement with this world's offers of contentment and comfort. Our calling in Rev 12:11,17 to witness boldly to the testimony of Jesus, will guarantee opposition from the Satanic powers. We must not fall into the trap of keeping our mouths shut and our Christian lives concealed. We must hold true at all times to the Lordship of Christ.

b. The End and the return of Christ will happen only after Jesus' disciples have fulfilled the Great Commission (Matt 24:14). Our goal as Christian believers is not to avoid or run away from pain, struggle or death, but rather to proclaim Jesus to this hostile but dying world (6:9-11; 11:3-7; 19:10). Yes, we must spiritually separate from worldly corruption, but not withdraw from sinners. Christians are meant to live godly lives in the in-between period between the first and second comings of Christ – the so-called already and the not yet! We have started to experience the life of the coming world, but we haven't yet entered it fully. Suffering will be ongoing in the spiritual warfare of this present life.

c. Serious willingness to evangelise the unsaved to the point of martyrdom will trigger the anger of Satan and his dark forces. They will hate and detest us, and we will need to ponder constantly that Jesus has indeed overcome the world (John 16:33). CS Keener (2000:330) quotes the example of Roman officials in Carthage ordering the execution of Perpetua as a young Christian woman. Perpetua had a vision of a ladder leading to heaven with a dragon at its foot –"He will not harm me, she said, in the name of Christ Jesus". "Then she stepped on his head and climbed up the ladder. Perpetua had understood this vision as the Lord's assurance that she would triumph through her martyrdom". She had shown that God's purposes are often achieved only through suffering and sometimes that will mean martyrdom.

d. Rev 12:7-9 declares spiritual warfare in the heavens that clearly corresponds to the victory and glorious triumph of Christ on the earth (12:5,10). It is *spiritual in nature.* However, it is not acceptable to ridicule the devil or address him as being present during a time of prayer. Christ has already won the warfare but much of this world has no awareness of this. Much of the world will readily believe in *virtually anything* rather than in the gospel of a crucified and risen Messiah! God is indeed sovereign and the devil's time is limited by God Himself. The kings and empires of this bodily world are merely pawns in the massive plan that God has.

e. We deal with the devil by delivering the oppressed and by proclaiming the gospel. As we prayerfully do this, God responds by removing the heavenly rulers. We overcome by the Word and in particular by the gospel. We must make *verbal witness for Jesus Christ.* Spiritual shortcuts will not work in warfare. Books of the Bible need to be treated seriously as wholes and parts, rather than as single verses. The parts need to be seen in relation to the whole and thus expounded as God intended. The great biblical scholar FF Bruce wrote, "Christians' only means of resisting the enemy's attack… is patient endurance and faithful confession. This may mean suffering and death; but it was precisely by suffering and death that their Leader has conquered." (*The Message of the NT* 1981:85). We can only ever test and prove the reality of our faith and endurance in the 'grinding machine' of real suffering. God is able to give us grace and strength to complete the race. He cares deeply for us – indeed, He died and rose for us.

f. Finally, and most importantly, we must learn to fight Satan *on a spiritual level, through the power of Word, Prayer and Holy Spirit.* If we rely on human effort or human will, we are sure to fail in spiritual warfare. Many Westerners tend to prioritise the physical, materialistic realm in life. The spiritual realm precedes, influences and to many degrees *decides* the physical realm. We need to seek to grasp just what is going on in the spiritual realm. In order to achieve this, we must hold firmly and constantly to our greatest spiritual reality, namely *the reality of Jesus Christ and our relationship with Him.* We also need to realise more fully that we must draw Jesus into the whole of life. The 'secular' must become spiritual, such that all of life is under the authority and control of the Godhead. Jesus' death, resurrection and reign must be current and contemporary in our daily lives *today.* The Holy Spirit makes this possible, powerful and real. He is the One who empowers and enables us, and He works in concert with the Word and with Prayer. Satan will always pull us away from Christ and from our personal relationship with Christ. True believers have a new mindset, a new nature, a new world and a new King who has defeated every authority and power. We are overcomers and we are victors ***through our union with Christ and our armour for warfare.***

Brief Bibliography on Spiritual Warfare

Biblical Exegesis

Check what standard commentaries on the Biblical Texts say about Spiritual Warfare, eg.

RT France on the Gospels of **Matthew** and **Luke**.

GK Beale's work on **Revelation**.

Check out Commentaries on **Ephesians**
eg by **Andrew Lincoln** or **FF Bruce,** especially Ephesians 6.

Books specifically on Spiritual Warfare

SHT Page, Powers of Evil – A Biblical Study of Satan and Demons, Baker Books, Grand Rapids, 1995.

Dr Ed Murphy, *Handbook for Spiritual Warfare,* Nashville: Thomas Nelson, 1992.

H Peskett and **V Ramachandra**, *The Message of Mission,* IVP: The Bible Speaks Today, 2003.

Hans Finzel, *The Top Ten Mistakes Leaders Make,* Cook Communications Ministries, Colorado, 2000.

DA Carson, *From Triumphalism to Maturity,* Baker Book House, 1984 and IVP, UK, 1988. Also Authentic Media Ltd, Milton Keynes, 2010.

Resources from Preachers' Gatherings:

by **C Peter White:**

- Preaching **Leviticus**
- Preaching **Deuteronomy**
- Preaching **Ezekiel**
- Preaching **Isaiah**
- Preaching **Song of Songs**

by **Derek Newton**

- Preaching **2nd Corinthians**
- Preaching **Colossians**
- Preaching **Hebrews**
- Preaching **James**
- Preaching **Revelation**
- Preaching **Spritual Warfare**

Available from

https://hearingtheword.org.uk

Initially, this work was divided into three booklets, delivered by Derek Newton at Preachers' Gatherings in Aviemore and Polmont, Scotland, November 2023.

First printed 18/8/2023 at Torrance Parish Church
1 School Rd, Torrance, Glasgow G64 BZ
Revised after the Gathering, 16/11/2023.
Revised for combined printing by Amazon, 13/6/2024

Printed in Great Britain
by Amazon

43848214R00066